The Musings of a Carolina Yankee

A Collection of Stories, Lies, and Other Weird Happenings

As Told by Wally Amidon

Biography & Autobiography - Personal Memoirs
Humor - General
Humor - Relationships

Second edition
Copyright 2014 by MSI Press, LLC

For information, contact
MSI Press
1760-F Airline Highway, #203
Hollister, CA 95023

Cover design by CDL Services

Cover photographs by Wally Amidon

Interior photographs:
    Part 1:   Carl D. Leaver
    Part 2:   Elzbieta Sekowska / Shutterstock.com
    Part 3:   Chiang Mai, Thailand / Shutterstock.com
    Part 4:   Ronald Sumners / Shutterstock.com
            Richard Scalzo / Shutterstock.com
            Ivan Marc / Shutterstock.com
            Carl D. Leaver

Library of Congress Control Number 2014948861

ISBN: 978-1-933455-96-9

Contents

Part 4
Observations on Life **103**

A Preface to the Craziness

People sometimes ask where I come up with the stories you are about to read on the following pages. I tell them there are four areas from which I draw my ideas:

1. just plain lies;

2. true things;

3. things that I wish were true and write them to sound true; and

4. sitting in front of my computer, writing these things, and actually believing them.

I guess some people dedicate their writings to people who have influenced their lives. I have to give credit, then, to Jeanne, my wife of 45 years, who has been my best friend since before marriage, and my two sons, Michael and Steven, who have kept me forever young at heart.

I can't leave out the people some of these stories are about, either. Without using them as a base to build upon, there would probably be a lot fewer words written here.

Finally, thanks to all the rednecks around the world. You don't have to be from the South to be a genuine redneck. Just be yourself, mind your own business, help others, and live life to the fullest. There will be someone out there, looking down on you because you have real values and morals. To them, you are a redneck, and I will love you for it.

Wally Amidon
Travelers Rest
South Carolina

Part 1
Of Nature, Animals, and Hunting

Wally Amidon

Alone in the Swamp

Have you ever had a day that you would like to forget but that seems to come back at regular intervals in your life to haunt you? I had such an adventure a few years back. I can laugh at it now, but at the time, it really tried my spirit.

I have two sons, Mike and Steven, who, I think, sometimes thought of themselves as Lewis and Clark because of the way they could navigate the woods. One day, they thought it would be nice to take me to their newly found hunting area. Now, things would have been different were I built more like a Chuck Norris or Sylvester Stallone, but I am built more for comfort than for physical exertion.

The boys came by the house at about 3:30 a.m. to pick me up for the adventure. I should have known the day was going to be long when they told me to hop into the back of the pickup as there wasn't enough room for the three of us in the front of the small truck they were driving. I loaded my stout frame into the back of the truck, and off we zoomed in the wee hours of the morning, headed to the great woods for a day of hunting for Bambi.

About an hour down the road, I felt something wet hit my face. Darn! It was beginning to rain. I started banging on the rear sliding window of the truck. One of the expedition leaders opened it and asked what I needed. I told him I was getting wet, and he said he would tell his brother to drive a little faster so the rain would fly over the windshield and hopefully exit near the tailgate. It wasn't working as the rain turned into a deluge. I was thinking I was going to begin to float out over the side of the truck bed if it came down any harder. I heard the truck begin to slow down a bit. My son Steven, who was driving, must have had pity on the old man in the back. I thought he was going to kick his older brother out of the front and let little poor ol' me get into the front where the heater was surging like a blast furnace in the steel mills of Pittsburgh. Wrong!!! He got out to tell me to wrap up in the tarp that was in the toolbox I was trying to seek refuge under. I got the tarp out and tried my best to make a co-coon out of it. I heard the truck begin to accelerate as Steven began shifting through the gears to hurtle us through the darkness of a wet South Carolina dawn.

All was going well under the tarp until I tried to turn over to get my hip bone off some foreign object left in the bed of the truck. Whatever it was, it felt like a harpoon slowly working itself into me, and the bumpy road wasn't helping much. As much I turned to get onto my back, the unthinkable happened. The wind caught the tarp and sent it flying free into the night air. I was going to knock on the back window again when I reasoned with myself that I would get a lot wetter if the truck stopped again and we had to back up and search along the road for my temporary shelter. I figured we could pick it up on the way back. I tried to crawl a little deeper under the toolbox but to no avail as I am about the size of the toolbox, which was bolted down to the truck bed. I pulled my collar up and tucked my head down into my coat, feeling like a scared turtle.

Finally, I felt us slowing down and figured we were taking a right turn as I slid across to the other side of the truck bed. I looked out of my temporary coat shelter and saw that the rain had abated and the first rays of the morning sun were trying to push their way through the grayness of the overcast sky.

I felt us slow to a stop and heard Steven switch the truck off as Mike jumped out of the passenger seat. "Where did the tarp go?" he asked as I tried to raise myself up to a half-sitting position.

I said, "That's another story, and we can get it on the way home if it's still there."

"That's okay," Mike said. "It was full of holes, and I was going to throw it away sometime this week." Go figure, I thought to myself as they opened the tailgate so I could make my agile exit.

I guess the boys knew the way down through the woods and didn't need Sacajawea to guide them. I was working hard, trying to keep up with them. Their legs must have grown longer than mine sometime in their life when I wasn't watching.

All was going well until we came to the creek and, like the Great Wallendas, they ambled across a fallen log, crossing like a couple of squirrels scampering through the woods. I put one foot on the log and looked down at the cold-looking creek, which was roaring and tearing along its course because of the heavy rain, about 12 feet below me.

"C'mon," the boys hollered simultaneously. "It's getting light, and we still have a ways to go."

I didn't want to lose the fearless image I had always tried to present to them as they were growing up, so I told them, "My boots are a little slippery, so I am going to sit down and scoot across the log so I don't fall into the creek."

I could see by the looks on their faces that they knew I was full of crap and wasn't going to take a chance on a plunge into the mini-Mississippi flowing below me. I sat on the log and began inching myself across. I should have looked a little closer at the log as along the way, just about the middle, I encountered green moss. Now, if you have ever felt green moss after a rain, you know that it holds water better than a sponge. As I tried to get across the moss, a wet, cold feeling began to sink in. That feeling was not in my mind. It was coming through the seat of my pants. Each pull across the moss probably squeezed an easy pint of water into my pants. I guess at about five gallons, I got to the end of the log and reached the safety of solid ground. My sons had possum looks on their faces as we trudged off. I'm sure I heard one of them say, "Hope he brought along some extra Depends for the rest of the day."

We walked along. Well, I should say, Mike and Steven walked along as I huffed and puffed about 50 yards to the rear. They would stop now and then to let me catch up, which I thought was nice, until I would finally reach them, and they would start walking again. I felt like the back part of a Slinky, never being able to keep up with the front.

After what felt like a 40-year wandering in the wilderness, we finally reached the place where the two explorers were going to drop me off for the day. They told me they would be along right after dark to retrieve me. Now, this was before the advent of cell phones. We had two-way radios, but they just didn't permeate the thickness of the forest where we were hunting.

The boys said that I would do well where they put me, to fire three shots in the air if I had any problems, and they would be right there to help me. I watched them leave and saw them walking at a rather quick pace, probably happy to have left the trailer behind. I watched them as they walked away and were slowly swallowed up by the thick vegetation.

The day passed without incident or sight of any deer. I did hear something coming toward me, rustling the leaves as it walked along. I readied my rifle and turned ever so slowly to see what I thought would be the trophy buck of a lifetime, only to find a skunk walking my way and pawing through the leaves, looking for insects. I kept a close eye on the polecat as he drew near. I slowly edged myself around the back of the tree I was sitting against, hoping to elude this hefty creature of fragrance. The skunk looked my way once and kept moving, probably not wanting to mess with a fat guy wearing wet britches.

The day slowly ebbed away, and darkness began to settle in. I thought I had better ready myself for when the boys returned and reached into my pack for my flashlight. I couldn't feel it in my pack, and my heart began to race a bit, thinking about sitting in the middle of a swamp, waiting in the dark for my two sons to come back and retrieve me.

The dark got darker, and I couldn't see three feet in front of me. I sat there with my back against a large yellow pine with my finger on the safety of my rifle, just waiting for something to jump out at me so I could let whatever it was have it. A crack of a limb behind me got my attention right quick as the safety went off, and my finger tightened around the trigger. I was letting myself feel like a little kid. It was actually fun for a few seconds at a time scaring myself and then snapping back into reality, knowing that there is nothing in the South Carolina woods that could hurt me—or was there?

I suddenly remembered tales of Lizard Man, who supposedly lurked in the swamps of South Carolina. Now, that couldn't be real, or could it? I thought to myself. The South Carolina Lottery Commission even ran an advertisement showing the creature in his swamp house, waiting for Powerball to come on so he could check his numbers. Nonsense, I thought to myself.

Crack! Another limb snapped. Whatever was making the noise was getting closer. I listened as I held my breath, hoping that whatever was lurking out there in the dark wouldn't hear my heavy breathing and the beating of my heart, which felt like it was going to launch through my chest and head into orbit. What are my kids going to say when they find my mangled corpse under the tree? What are they going to tell their mother, or would they even bother telling her? Now, that thought got me going, and my bravery returned like that of a barfly who threatened to take on the world when he couldn't stand straight enough to do it without falling flat on his face.

"I'll fix them if they don't tell her or make up some kind of story that I went down like a champion fighting rather than trying to bury myself a little deeper into the forest floor," I muttered to myself, being careful to make sure I wasn't loud enough for the monster in the woods to hear me.

"Yea, though I walk," I was saying when I realized I wasn't walking but pressed close to the ground, peering into the ink beyond. I wonder if that prayer covers people who are trying to hide from murderous creatures, I thought to myself.

I could hear whatever it was coming closer and closer. I took my hunting knife from the sheath, held it in my right hand, and clutched my rifle in my left hand. Whatever this demon was preying on me was going to suffer agony from multiple stab and rifle wounds. Come on, big boy, I thought to myself. My bravery level was even with my fear level now. I felt bi-polar. Scared, then brave, then scared, then brave again. I was hoping for the best and that the brave part would outlast the scared part—just a few seconds longer.

Now, I could hear footsteps behind me. Darn! That stinking monster had outflanked me and was coming in for the kill. Did I want to turn, face my attacker like a man, and go out in a blaze of glory, or was I going to cower, trembling like a babbling idiot, and be ripped to shreds without putting up a fight? Thoughts of Davy Crockett at the Alamo, swinging Ol' Betsy and trying to take out as many as he could before he would be slain in a hopeless battle fluttered through my tortured brain. The Davy Crockett song started running through my mind as the steps in the dark drew closer to the place that would be memorialized as my final stand.

I could hear all four feet shuffling through the leaves and cracking little sticks on the ground as I readied myself for eternity. I peered into the darkness, trying to see some type of outline or shape, but it was just too dark. I felt my heart racing and thought to myself that these were the final beats I would ever hear. My life was beginning to flash before me when a light suddenly flashed into my face.

It was Michael and Steven. Hallelujah! God is still on the throne! My kids have come to rescue their poor old dad. "Are you ready?" one of the boys asked.

I replied, "Sure. Why didn't you use your light when you were walking through the woods so I could have seen you coming a lot sooner?"

My son replied, "Our batteries were dying, and we know our way around these woods, anyhow. Why waste them? We will need the lights to get you back across the log." I had forgotten about my return Grand Canyon crossing but was ready for anything after the ordeal I had just suffered.

"How come you had your knife out?" my eldest asked.

"Oh, I was just whittling while waiting for you guys to come get me." I don't think they believed me as there were no shavings or sticks nearby, but they didn't say anything.

"Did you see anything today?" I asked as we walked through the darkness.

"Nope" was the reply, "but we did hear something big running through the woods when we got close to where you were sitting. Did you see anything?"

"Nope," I said as I hastened my pace and got into second place in the line.

We finally made it back to the truck after what seemed to be an eternity of walking. I got across the log all right and wasn't caring much about the mini-Colorado River raging below. My mind had been on what I was leaving behind more than falling off the log and into the thundering abyss below. I had escaped alive from the creature lurking in the depths of the swamp. I was ready for the ride back home and to let the jitters settle some.

I found my place in the back of the truck and cuddled myself into the corner to keep the wind off me. My boys stopped to look for the tarp, but it was gone. Somebody probably saw it and picked it up. We rattled long the road for a few minutes, and I decided to roll over on my back. I had just gotten into a comfortable position, pulled my pack up for a pillow, and closed my eyes when the first drop of rain hit me on the side of my face.

Storm Driving

I was following Mike home from working on food plots all day one Saturday. It was absolutely beautiful outside. So, I rolled down the driver and passenger side windows on the Jeep. Willie was singing away on the radio. A perfect end to a good day!

We were tooling along at 60, with wind tiptoeing through the window, sun on the road, and song in the heart (and ears). As soon as we got to Woodruff Road, though, traffic slowed down to 35 all of a sudden, and the skies burst open as if someone had opened a celestial shower full spigot. Flood II had started!

I looked up the road, and a curtain of rain was coming our way. As it approached, lightning began hitting all around us. Very quickly, it sounded like the 1810 Overture outside my windows. It was loud, really loud, like gunshots coming from the back seat. I jacked the radio up and kept my speed at a level 45 mph until I got on the other side of that curtain.

On the other side of Greenville, the other side of the curtain, that is, everything was dry. I cleaned the mud off the Jeep, trailer and four-wheeler.

Thanks, Lord, for the wash job on everything! It saved me from having to take out the pressure washer and clean everything off.

I never did stop to zip up the windows. The cool spray felt good after a long day in the hot sun.

Two Hunters

I had a red fox come visit me at my ground blind one evening. He came close, sat down in the road, and watched me.

Every now and then, he would turn his head and look about. He scratched some fleas a few times, got up, and started sniffing the air.

I took my rifle and looked at him through the cross hairs. Then, I zoomed in on him but, for some reason, stopped and watched for a while. The season was open on them, but I asked myself why I should kill this pretty creature. I was not going to put him in the freezer, and his fur looked better on him than hanging on my wall.

He stayed for about 20 minutes and then walked on down the road. He stopped midway, sat down in the road, and looked back up to where I was sitting and watching him. He was never afraid although he kept his distance. He let me watch him in his own living room.

It makes a hunter realize who he truly is when he doesn't gun down everything he sees just because he can. I am sitting in my easy chair, writing this, and I am sure that fox is out there, hunting for supper.

Two hunters got to meet one another and parted company. Both were happy with the results.

Some Realities of Hunting

In hunting, there are some realities. Call them realities of life, if you like. If you are not a hunter, you don't know them. So, I am listing some of them here for you along with real-life examples.

Priorities

One Sunday during our morning church service, our pastor was dealing with priorities. Jokingly, he singled out the hunters in the congregation to ask us what time we had to get up to go hunting. "What time do you have to get up?" he asked me. "Round about 3:30," I responded. Others had other predawn rising times.

The pastor was using this as an example of commitment. I didn't have the heart to tell him that by 7:30, I could be found sound asleep in my deer stand, wrapped up in a wool blanket and trying keeping warm. That is the rest of the story.

Early Closure

One year, I had taken the day off for the last day of deer season—and the day before found out that they were closing deer season a day early. That is like going to your wedding and finding out your bride's -father switched the love of your life with her ugly, cross-eyed, heifer-looking sister. I needed intensive therapy after hearing that devastating news.

Pretension

Some time ago, I was watching the hunting channel. This guy was sitting in a heated blind. He had just described all of his over-priced hunting gear. He said he had been hunting hard. Does that make sense to you?

Later in the show, one of his buddies arrowed a deer, and immediately rock music came blaring out of nowhere. I wonder if he had to pay those band members to sit out in the cold until he shot a deer, or do you think he was cheating with canned music?

Missing Teeth

At one point, I had over two hundred pounds of West Virginia deer to cut and grind in the coming week. My two sons and friend, Mike, had thinned the herd up there. Mike noticed that the does were missing a lot of teeth. I was not surprised. Well, they were West Virginia deer, weren't they?

Season's End

After a season of hunting, I got to the woods one final time. It is good that the season was drawing to close. I was beginning to look like something that lives out in the wild.

Ticks

When I got back home one night after a day of hunting, my wife told me to take off my shirt to see if I had picked up any ticks down in the woods while out there. When she wasn't looking, I put a watermelon seed under my arm. When I lifted my arm up, she saw it. Don't ask me how I got this black eye, either. She doesn't like ticks— or watermelon seeds used to scare her.

Snow

Last year, they said there was a chance of snow on one Saturday afternoon here in South Carolina. Well, all the deer rifles were still loaded and ready to go. Brown against a white background would have been something I hadn't seen since I had left New Hampshire 28 years earlier. It ought to be interesting, I thought.

And, oh, yes, the anti-aircraft gun was still loaded and ready for Christmas Eve. Ah, the smell of reindeer roasts in. the smoker!

A Christmas Story

It was the day of Christmas Eve. I had been deer hunting with my son and a friend of his. The friend shot a nice little buck with a fair, but not large-sized, rack. My son asked if I might take it down to the local processor for them as they had to pack their things up and get ready to head home. I agreed to do so.

There I was, driving along the highway in my little, red, '94 Toyota half-ton pickup, dressed somewhat like Santa. My son and his friend were ahead of me in their truck. I had my ATV on the back of the truck with the friend's buck strapped to the rack so it would be easy to take off at the processor's. I noticed a lot of people were driving by and giving me dirty looks. I thought they were incensed about a deer being on an ATV. Times are a-changin', I thought to myself, but who cares. This is how we did it back in my day.

A car full of little kids pulled even with me, and the little kids were going crazy. Some of them even looked like they were going to go into shock. Am I that stunning—or ugly? I thought to myself. The mother poked her head out the window, yelled something in Spanish, and shook her fist at me.

I rolled down the window and yelled out, "Feliz Navidad!" That is about all the Christmas Spanish I know. She yelled out some other Spanish words that I didn't understand, and her husband gave me the international finger salute. I didn't know what they were so upset about and figured they were learning how to be decent American citizens.

A trucker gave me thumbs up a few minutes later and blared his air horn as he rolled by. I almost filled my Christmas stockings when I first heard the air horn blaring. I didn't know what it was or where it was coming from.

I called the guys on my cell phone and told them I had to stop for gas and would meet them at the processor's in a few minutes. They were laughing about something as they drove on, and I turned off at the next exit to gas up the little, red Toyota.

I was just about finished filling the gas tank when this crazy woman came up, yelling, "How could you be so cruel and especially at this time of year?"

I was thinking to myself, okay, not another anti-hunting nut, and here I am dressed partially as Santa. How am I going to calm her down and explain the ethics of hunting to her without being clobbered by the duffel-bag-sized purse she had slung over her shoulder. I calmly told her that deer hunting was part of my heritage and that I was not some kind of bloodthirsty fanatic out using God's creatures as living targets to satisfy my bloodthirsty urges.

She replied, "My husband and I hunt deer, too, but we don't do this to the deer, especially on Christmas Eve."

I asked, "What are you talking about?"

She went ballistic, grabbed me by the beard, and led me to the back of my truck where the deer was tied to the rack on my ATV. She asked, "Haven't you got any feelings for anyone but yourself? Don't you care that little children will see this and be disturbed?"

My mind went back to the little kids I saw in the car a few miles back and the hard looks they had given me. I asked the lady, who was now snorting like a raging bull, what I had done besides having a dead deer strapped to an ATV on the back of my truck.

"This, you &%$#*!" she screamed as she pointed toward the deer. Oh, no! I had been set up by two elves who had me wear the Santa hat and then left me to myself at the gas station. There on the back of my ATV was a nice buck whose nose had been spray painted with red paint.

One of those bums had diverted my attention with the Santa hat while the other one got to the back of the truck and did the heinous deed of spraying the deer's nose with red paint. I told the lady someone had done that to make me look bad. She looked me over from head to toe and screamed, "You don't need any help in that area!" Then, she stormed back to her VW Beetle and screeched her tires on the way out of the parking lot.

I found some paper towels and wrapped them around the deer's nose and tied them on with a bungee cord I had on the ATV. Needless to say, when I finally got to the processor, the culprits were nowhere to be found, but the owner greeted me with, "Well, hello, Santa! Did you bring Rudolph with you?"

Emma's Britches

I went down to the hunt club the other day to do a little muzzleloader hunting. We have lanes that head to out entrance gates. I found a pair a ladies used (that's not the word) britches flung up into a tree by one of the main gates. Probably got there when she and her boyfriend began whatever they were doing down there, and that wasn't having a poker game. I looked at them fluttering in the wind and tried to figure out just how big this woman had to be. I got a long stick and knocked them onto the ground. They were the size of a deflated weather balloon. I didn't have a shovel to bury them with as I would have had to dig a rather large pit for them. I had a bright idea, though. I put on a pair of rubber gloves, hitched a cord to them, and drug them the length of the road to my deer stand, thinking maybe a buck would get the scent and come charging in.

Once I got to my stand, I drove past it and down the road a quarter mile, then tossed the britches under my buddy's stand. I got back to my stand, and I waited for an hour or so. Nothing came. All of a sudden, I heard this loud grunting coming down the road. I quickly threw off the safety and was waiting for Big Nasty to come into view after following the scent from Mama Nasty's drawers.

I was waiting, and the Thompson Center Black Diamond was waiting to spew fire and lead. The grunting slowed and finally came to a stop. I waited and waited and could hear this strange purring-like sound. Then, the grunting started again and stopped again. The purring sound was getting closer. I wondered what could be making that sound. Finally, I saw something rounding the corner in the road by the food plot. It was a huge, feral hog with a younger one in tow. They were following the britches trail and snorting. They would stop and roll on the scent trail, making that funny purring sound, then get up and start snorting again as they followed the trail. I was going to take a shot but passed. I didn't want to break up their fun.

I guess they must have come to the end of the trail under my buddy's stand and found what they had been lusting after. I heard all kinds of commotion coming from that direction: squealing, snorting, and purr-like noises. They must have been fighting over the newfound treasure because they were tearing the place up. They left after a while, and I started to sneak down there to see what they had been doing.

My buddy had come in from the other direction, and he and the hogs had come upon the britches at the same time. I saw my buddy. He looked like he had been rolling in the mud and had tears in his clothes. He really looked like the hogs had gotten the best of him. He saw me standing there, looking at him, and said, "Them hogs had Emma's britches, and I had to get them back. We were carrying on in the parking lot the other night, and she hung them in a tree. I told her I would get them on the way out after hunting. I came in here, and them hawgs had 'em and were rolling around on them. I didn't have my gun with me, so I cut a stick and went after them. It took some doin', but I finally got 'em away from 'em. Wonder how them hawgs got up in that tree to get 'em?"

I never said a word as I walked off, laughing to myself. I was almost back to my stand when I suddenly woke up. It had been a nightmare. I was glad it was because I wouldn't ever do anything like that with Emma's britches to a feral hog.

The Rat Dog

Have you ever seen something and wondered to yourself—or out loud—why God ever created it? I have wondered this myself and have written a short story about a creation that has brought joy, pain, fear, and terror to various members of our little family.

My son and his wife wanted the ultimate pet and decided upon a Jack Russell Terrier. They wanted a Jack Russell because this breed is supposed to be small but fierce defenders of the domain. They got a deal on the puppy they brought home because it was the runt of the litter. *Runt* isn't really the word. I really believe they bought Baby Satan in a small-dog costume. This clown acts like a mosquito on crack.

When we go over to their house to visit, Rat Dog thinks the visit is for her and for the two humans she lets live in her house. You see, Rat Dog took over as soon as she moved in. The only good thing I can see here is that they lock the little demon in a cage so she can't tear things up. All she wants is to lock her jaws onto something and have you take it away from her. She will lock her legs and shake her head, trying to dislodge what she has offered you in the tug-of-war.

I had the unfortunate occasion to be sitting on the couch and letting my guard down while visiting over there one day. I was sprawled haphazardly across the couch, having taken my eyes off Rat Dog for a split second. That was all it took for Rat Dog to spring into her Mighty Dog act. She leapt off the couch on the other side of the room, hit the coffee table in between the couches, and launched herself at me like a guided missile with snapping teeth. I happened to look up just in time to see the demon hurtling through the air with fangs bared. Before I could raise my arms in defense, the critter was attempting a nipple pierce at my expense.

I grabbed the little sausage by the head and pulled her off me. I tossed her like a pregnant football back to the other couch. She hit the couch, bounced off the back cushions, and launched herself once again.

This time I was prepared. I caught her in mid-air before she could strike again. I think this surprised her since she calmed down. I released her. That was the second mistake I made that day.

She came running back to me with what was left of a stuffed squirrel my son had bought her a few days prior to my visit. It looked like a piece of gray cloth. There was no shape left to the once cuddly little stuffed animal that had been presented as a toy to Canine Caligula just the day before. It had been ripped to shreds. I surveyed what was left of the squirrel and quickly covered my chest, thinking that Rat Dog was feigning a time to play only to get close enough for a chance at another attack upon me.

I covered my chest with my arm as Rat Dog offered me the rest of what had been her toy. I took hold of the fabric. It was wet and cold. This critter had been chewed like it had been through a meat tenderizer. I held onto my end of the squirrel while Rat Dog shook her head from side to side, trying to get it away from me. I held Rat Dog off the floor, cocking my arm like a brace for support. She hung in space for over ten minutes, growling and trying to kick at me, all the time squinting at me with her beady, little, brown eyes, hoping I would loosen my grip so she would be the victor.

I finally gave up as it was like trying to hold a truck battery suspended in air for a duration of over ten minutes. Thinking she had won, Rat Dog began parading back and forth before me. I wanted to pretend I was stretching and kick the little hag across the room, but my son was there, watching the parade and laughing at what Rat Dog had put me through that afternoon. How could I kick his pride and joy? Even his wife wasn't allowed to seek vengeance against this little monster.

She finally got tired of her little parade and jumped up on the back of the couch, pretending she wanted to be friends. I knew she wanted to grab my ear so I kept my distance.

Rat Dog saw my wife enter the living room. She was wearing a dress. Rat Dog ran up under the dress and tried to snap at whatever she could get hold of under the dress. My wife was a-hollering. Rat Dog had bitten into the inside of the dress and was holding on like a snapping turtle. Now, this was funny for two reasons: first, to see my wife trying to get Rat Dog from under the dress, and second, because it wasn't happening to me. My son finally pried Demon Dog from his mother, took the monster back into the bedroom, and locked her in her cell.

I guess I should tell the reader that Rat Dog has a real name. They call her Jackie, short for Jacqueline. That critter ain't no Kennedy; that's for sure. They can call her nice names, but I refer to the Hound from Hell as Fang.

I still say I can see three 6s faintly inscribed in the mutt's skull, but they say I am making it up because I think she is possessed. I fully expect to go over there some day and see that thing turn her head a full 360 degrees and start puking green pea soup. Until then, I never venture over there without wearing my trusty Kevlar t-shirt.

Eagle Lake Fishing Trip

In the course of a man's life, there comes a time to think back to simpler times and things that made you a little happier as the years rolled by. One of these snippets involved my father-in-law, Louis Saucier.

The story begins in Eagle Lake, Maine, where Louis was born and grew up. Part of the family journeyed back to the homeland with him from our home in New Hampshire to visit his relatives and to do a little fishing.

At this time, Eagle Lake was still a small town, made up mostly of small houses and camps. It was a place that appeared to be in lost in time. The inhabitants neither realized this nor particularly cared about it. Most of them were family in some way or related to others who were related to someone in the town. I would venture to say that this was where the term, *close-knit family*, came from.

I had never before been to Eagle Lake, nor had I met this side of the family. It was fun from the get-go. When we arrived, people came out of the house, speaking Canadian French in rapid bursts. I tried to figure out what they were saying since I had taken French in high school but to no avail. They had their own dialect. I knew it would be a fruitless effort when I heard the New Hampshire side of the family reply to the Eagle Lake side of the family in a French language that had English words mixed into the sentences because the French vocabulary had escaped the speakers since they moved south and began losing their rich, deep-woods culture. I listened as my father-in-law and his brothers grew hoarse, yelling at one another in the Canadian French and American French dialects. Later, I found out they were not yelling but just talking naturally as time working around heavy machinery had taken its toll on their hearing. This was an exercise in listening, to say the least.

After a lunch consisting of potatoes and meat that Louis's sister, Marie, told us was not "store meat," the men began to plot the fishing trip. I didn't use the word *plan* as it really wouldn't fit in this story. *Plot* was more like it as those involved in the trip itinerary were haggling on which place would be best to fill the fishing creels that next morning. After about an hour, they had settled on where we were going to go. I knew half of the story only because of the few English words I heard and knitted them into what I thought were sentences they may have been saying. Everyone there could speak good English, but they were reliving the "old days" before they had to learn the city-people language.

Being there that first day, I realized why my father-in-law was who he really was. I was in his "country," where the air was fresh and clean, the water crystal clear, and the people innocent and friendly. People made you feel as if you were one of them and would even smile at dumb jokes told to them that they did not really understand or did not really think were funny. I say all of the above to get the person reading this to be able to understand the rest of the story.

We woke the following morning to the smell of breakfast being prepared by "Ma Tante Marie," as she was affectionately called by the rest of the family. For the English-speaking reader, this translates to "My Aunt Marie." We all sat around the table, and she loaded down with enough food to feed a crew of lumberjacks. There were things on that table that I had never seen or tasted before, but it was all good—and I am still alive to write this.

Breakfast being finished, we loaded whoever could fit into my Jeep. The rest followed in an old pickup truck. Just before we left, I saw Louis catch a cricket and put it into his shirt pocket. I didn't ask him about the cricket as I knew he would tell me later. We fished some of the streams closer to town and did well, but my father-in-law said we would do better at this place he knew deep in the woods. He told me the name of the place, but I will never be able to pronounce the name, let alone figure out how to spell it. We were traveling a dirt road that seemed to have no end.

We would stop at little tributaries that most people would walk or drive by without a second thought. Louis, though, would tap my shoulder and say, "Stop here!" Then, he would get out of the Jeep, take his fishing line (he didn't take a pole), and soon come walking back with a branch full of trout. There were so many fish in the waters up there in the woods that they rarely grew more than six inches in length, and Louis was piling up the numbers.

As we were driving down the road, we rounded a corner, and he told me to stop and for everyone to be quiet. I watched him as he got out of the Jeep, walked quietly down the road to a spot about 50 yards away, and then suddenly stopped. He reached into his pocket, took out the cricket, and attached it to the hook on the fish line he was carrying. He slowly lowered the bait to the road. As I watched, I asked myself what he was doing dropping that cricket onto the ground with a fish line. Suddenly, I saw him jerk the line and pull a huge brook trout out of the middle of the road. I drove up to him and saw that he had dropped his line into a hole in a culvert which crossed the road. The fish he caught was magnificent. It had bright spots and a bright red belly and was bent like a ripe banana. It was close to 11 inches long—a real trophy. Louis held it up for all of us to see. He had his trophy and was beaming from ear to ear.

As we were heading back down that lonely, logging road that evening, I looked over at my father-in-law. He had his bag of fish that he had caught throughout the day, and the trophy was on top as if he wanted to look down occasionally and make sure it was still there. His fishing rod was coiled and on the floor board of the Jeep. He drifted off into a light sleep as we traveled along. I wondered what he might be dreaming about. Was it a dream of years ago when he wandered this wilderness as a boy, carefree, catching fish in the cold, clear streams, chasing deer through the dense, dark forests, and leading a similar type of life? Or was it something that somebody who wasn't born there couldn't quite understand. The one thing I could really bet on and win was that he was dreaming in the language of his boyhood in the deep woods of Maine.

Part 2
People I Have Known

Wally Amidon

Bingo Drake

I heard the following story told this way, and I will not try to embellish or otherwise deviate from the way I heard it. That is on purpose.

The story takes place somewhere in Appalachia, back up in the hills, a few miles after the roads stop and the trails to the cabins start to get narrower. There was a boy living back there in the hills; his name was Bingo Drake. Now, the Drake family and their descendants had been living in that part of the mountains since Daniel Boone dropped them off on his way to the Kentucky frontier. There is no explanation about why old Daniel left them by the wayside, but as the story goes, it was for some major infraction of frontier living rules.

Bingo's father said he named him Bingo because he was the fifth son born straight in a row in a family of 14 children. Bingo was a little different from the rest of his siblings. While his brothers and sisters spent their spare time whittling, making corn husk dolls and the like, Bingo spent the majority of his time throwing rocks at things. After a couple of years, he was getting pretty accurate. His fame began to spread throughout the mountains, and he was becoming a legend among his own. Bingo would win turkey shoots by throwing rocks at the critters rather than using a rifle, which he thought was expensive. "Why, heck," he would say to others, "why spend money on a rifle and then have to make or buy the bullets when all this natural, God-given ammunition (rocks) are lying here like manna from Heaven. All ya have to do is warm up yore rock pitchin' arm a bit and let 'er rip. After a while, you can get them rocks down range with both eyes open, and you will be hunting fer nothin."

Yes, Bingo's reputation was legendary, so legendary, in fact, it crept out of the mountains and into one of the small towns below. It seems that a baseball scout was passing through the town of Seed Tick one day and happened to stop at the little general store on the edge of town to pick up a RC Cola and a Moon Pie. Now, if you are from that part of the woods, an RC Cola and a Moon Pie were mighty fine eatin' and made the list of local favorite cuisine in just about every home along the way.

It was a rather warm day, and the baseball scout was sitting on a bench outside the door, waiting for a breeze to pass by while patting the sweat from his face with an oversized white handkerchief and feasting on the diet of the mountain gods. While sitting there, he overheard (not really overheard, as he was really straining to listen in) a couple of the locals talking about the exploits of Bingo Drake.

The baseball scout edged over a little closer and asked the men, "Is this Bingo feller good with a baseball?"

Now, this brought guffaws from the two locals. One of them spoke up and said, "Up there where Bingo lives, there ain't no level place to play a game like that. If you try to catch a ball and it gets by you, it will roll plumb down into the valley below, and nobody is dumb enough to play a game that involves running up and down the mountain, chasing a baseball. Now, don't get me wrong, Mister. If'n you want to do something like that, then you can have at it. Us mountain people just don't think that's a way to spend your time when you can be huntin', fishin', or shinin'."

The scout didn't dare ask what *shinin'* was all about. It could be holding a light on a deer after dark or something to do with a still— and he certainly wasn't going to bring up that subject since he was a stranger with out-of-state plates on his car.

The scout gathered up his things and asked them men where he might find Bingo Drake. "Up there somewhere," one of them said, pointing to the mountains outside of town. "He lives up there with his mother, father, and 13 brothers and sisters. It hain't hard to find. Just foller the road outta town and take the right fork when you cross the river. Foller the road until it stops. You can park your car there. Nobody will steal your gas 'cause nobody up there has a car to put it in. Git on the trail, and keep on a-takin' the trails that go to the right. Git up the hill some, and cross the little bridge that goes over the creek. It's only three miles up the mountain from the bridge. You can't miss the place. The trail stops there, and you will hear all those kids just a-havin' fun up there."

The scout took off, thinking to himself that these local yokels thought he was gullible enough to believe a story like they had just told him. He was about a mile down the road and tempted to turn back and sneak into town just to hear if they were sitting on the bench out front of the store laughing about the misdeed they had just done to this outside city slicker, but the afternoon was drawing on and he wanted to find the Drake place before dark. The longer he drove up into the mountains, the more his heart began to sink within him. "Maybe they were right and weren't lying to me about where the Drake place is. I sure hope they were exaggerating a little bit about the length of the walk into the place."

He followed the road until it ended, just as the local had told him. As he got out of his car, he looked at his watch. "I have about five good hours of daylight left. I better take my flashlight, just in case," he said to himself as he drew an oversized handkerchief out of his pocket and wiped the perspiration from his wrinkled brow.

The scout followed the trail. He walked and walked and finally found the little bridge, which actually was not a bridge at all but a log felled across the creek. Now, this scout wasn't one of the Wallendas and wasn't going to take a chance of slipping off the log and falling into the creek, so he sat on the log and began to pull himself across. "Wrong idea," he said to himself as the first splinter from the log lodged itself deep in his inner thigh. He tried backing up, but another shard found a place to bury itself in his hind side. Now, he was stuck between two splinters.

"Well," he thought to himself as he tried to raise himself up off the log, "there is only one way out of this." The splinters had him pretty much stuck on the log. The scout gave a final thrust straight up as the splinters broke off within him. He yelled so loud it sounded as if someone were skinning a mountain lion alive. The echo of his scream was broken only by the sound of a loud splash as he hit the icy cold mountain water five feet below the log. Someone should have been there with a camera as he was out of that creek quicker than a house cat and heading up the trail at a fast trot toward the Drake cabin.

The handkerchief turned into a bandanna as the scout huffed and puffed his way the remaining three miles of the trail, all the time thinking to himself that Audie Murphy really didn't know what it was really like to go "To Hell and Back." He kept on while humming the theme to *Rocky* to himself and thinking of himself as a mighty victor, ready to conquer this wilderness that was trying to swallow him alive. Finally, he rounded a corner and saw a little cabin built on the side of the mountain.

There were children of all ages engaged in one form of chore or another. With 14 helping hands, chore time was short. The scout straightened up and took a few quick breaths as he neared the cabin. He removed the bandanna from this head as he didn't want his first appearance to be met with some concern from Papa Drake, as he was known to the locals, as to why he climbed a mountain with a rag on his head. Surely, he did not want anyone even to think he was an unhealthy city slicker, huffing and puffing his way up the trail.

For some strange reason, none of the children paid any attention to him as he walked through their midst. One of them did say to his brother, "That guy pulled himself across the log."

His little brother asked, "How you know that?"

The older brother laughed and pointed at the scout's pants. "Look at them splinters stickin' outta his butt." They both laughed and continued on doing what mountain kids do.

The scout got to the front of the cabin and found Papa Drake rocking in his rocking chair and whittling a model of a mule out of a piece of hemlock.

"You Mr. Drake?" asked the scout.

Papa Drake continued rocking, spit the chew drippings from his lower lip, and answered, "Yep." You see, in the mountains it isn't polite to talk when you have a mouth full of chew drippings.

"And who might you be?" asked Papa Drake as he eyed the scout up and down.

The scout replied, "I'm Ray Davis. I'm a scout."

Papa Drake quit rocking, chewing, and whittling at the same time and asked, "What you scoutin'? Everything around here is pretty much found."

The scout replied, "No, I am not that kind of scout. You see, I'm a baseball scout, and I heard one of your sons has a pretty good arm when throwing. I would like to talk to him some if that's all right with you. I just want to see his stuff."

"What you mean, 'see his stuff'?" Papa Drake said angrily as he rose from the rocking chair. "What kind of pervert be you, Mister? Maw, git the shotgun. We got one of them pettyfilers out here a-wantin' to see Bingo's stuff."

"No, no," screamed the scout. "What I meant was, see how he can throw."

Papa Drake took the shotgun from his wife, who had her finger on the hammer of the antiquated weapon, and said "You better say what you mean the first time you say something 'round here, Mister. We don't take to people wantin' to see our kids' stuff."

Saved from two barrels of buckshot, the scout explained his purpose for coming to the Drake cabin and told Papa Drake that maybe Bingo might have a chance to leave the mountain for the big leagues.

"Big leagues?" queried Papa Drake. "What are those?"

"Well, you might say it is getting to the top."

Papa Drake looked the scout over and asked, "Speakin' of gittin' to the top, how did you git across the log at the creek? Now, don't say you walked across 'cause I see the splinters hangin' outta yore backside. Maw, fetch the snips. I gotta help this poor guy out. He drug his butt across the log and has about a cord of splinters in him. Nothin' worse than splinters where you can't reach 'em , 'cept mebbe when a porkypine gits hold a ya. Now, bend on over, and let me have at 'em. "

The scout bent over, and a dreadful thought went through his mind. What are the 'ems he's talking about. Surely, he isn't talking about the family jewels. He wasn't serious when he thought I was after his kid's "stuff," was he? I only have costume jewelry at best.

Papa Drake got hold of one of the splinters, and then quickly kicked the scout on the seat of the pants, sending him sprawling face down into the yard. "Git back up here, and we'll git the othern."

The scout once again submitted himself this weird way of pulling splinters. "I only do it that way so's it doesn't hurt when the splinter comes out. You only think about the heel of my boot on your back-side, and the splinter part don't come to mind."

"Okay, I guess, if that's the way you really do it up here," said the scout as he dusted himself off after the second splinter had been yanked from his backside.

The two little miscreants mentioned earlier in this story were hiding on the side of the house, just having a good laugh. "Look at that guy," said the eldest. "Papa kicks him in the butt, and he thanks him for it. Strange people, them city people."

"Where might I find Bingo?" asked the scout.

Papa Drake looked about and cocked his head a bit. "He's down there in the holler, squirrel huntin' for Maw. See, Maw makes this lip-smackin' Brunswick Stew with the squirrels Bingo brings back. He ought to be back soon. Maw only needed a dozen or so."

"Well, just point the way, Mr. Drake, and I'll head out and find him."

Papa Drake pointed to a grove of oak trees about 500 yards down the mountain. "Head that way, but be quiet. He's a huntin', and you don't want to scare everything off."

"Okay, I'll do that," said the scout as he ambled off down the side of the mountain.

It wasn't long before he stumbled onto Bingo. Bingo had about a dozen squirrels slung over his shoulder and was looking up in the trees for more of the bushy-tailed quarry. Bingo spied the scout long before the scout saw him and only showed himself to see what he wanted.

"Hi, there," said the scout as he walked up to Bingo. "Fine bunch of squirrels you have there. I hear you throw rocks at them, and I came up here to see how well you did it."

"Shucks, ain't nothin' to it," said Bingo as he picked up a rock about the size of a tennis ball and looked up into a tall oak.

"Here, watch this," he said as he hurled the tock up into the tree. A loud thump was heard, and a squirrel fell dead at the scout's feet.

"That's amazing," said the scout. "How did you learn to do that?"

"It come easy to me," said Bingo. "I had 12 years of practice before I started huntin' these here woods."

"How old are you, son?" asked the scout.

"I reckon I'll be 14 come winter," said Bingo.

"That's amazing!" said the scout, sensing the money to be made with this young hurler who wasn't even old enough to sign a contract on his own, let alone know what a contract was. The scout followed Bingo along as he used the same rock to kill three more squirrels.

"I have to go now, but you're welcome to follow along,"

The scout was amazed at what he had been seeing, but something just wasn't right, he thought as he walked. Then, it dawned on him. Bingo had been knocking squirrels out of trees with the accuracy of a Marine sniper, only he was using rocks. He never missed, but that wasn't the point. The scout finally remembered what he wanted to ask Bingo.

"Bingo," he asked, "I have been watching you hurl rocks into trees this afternoon. You never miss, and you throw the rocks like guided missiles. I have just one question because I must have misunderstood what I was hearing. I heard you were a right-hander."

"That I am, sir," replied Bingo.

"But you are so accurate throwing with your left hand. Why don't you throw right-handed?"

Bingo paused, looked the scout in the face, and said, "'Cause Papa says I throw too hard right-handed, and I tend to spoil a lot of meat."

Christmas Eve 1969

Christmas Eve 1969 found me on a secluded mountaintop radar site, located on what was then the East German border. I had married the love of my life a few days earlier on the 13th, and then my orders came to report to Germany. There wasn't much to do at a place like this unless you liked skiing, and skiing and I never got along. Most of the guys spent their time in the NCO/Officers' Club, sipping German beer and talking among themselves. Christmas was on the brink, and most thoughts were on the folks we had left behind in the States.

I went into the NCO Club and looked around. I thought to myself as I looked at the guys sitting about: here we are, a bunch of kids, stuck on this mountain, waiting for a war to begin.

Outside, the wind was blowing, and there was a hint of snow in the air. I looked to the east, and I could see the Russian/East German observation posts rising into the skyline a few miles away. I wondered what those guys did on Christmas since Communists were not to believe in God or recognize any religious holidays.

As evening approached, one of my buddies asked what I was going to be doing on Christmas Eve. I told him I didn't really have any plans or money since my pay orders had not yet arrived. He smiled, handed me a five-dollar bill, and said, "Merry Christmas, and don't worry about getting it back to me. We all watch over each other up here." That sentence stuck with me the whole time I was there.

I went back to the barracks and was heading up to my room when one of the German border guards asked me what I was going to be doing Christmas Eve night. I told him I would probably head over to the NCO Club later on and join the rest of the guys. He said, "You can come along with us for four hours. We have border patrol from eight until midnight. If you want to go with us, I will get it cleared."

I told him I would like to go. I had not yet seen the border up close, and this would be a great opportunity. I went to my room, changed into my fatigues (BDUs today), went to the section of the barracks where the German guards lived, and waited.

Soon, I saw three guards in full battle dress and with UZI machine guns heading my way. I saw the guard I had met earlier, and he said, "We have a truck outside. My name is Schmidt."

He then introduced the two others. One was named Neuhaus and the other Schonburg. I walked down the barracks hall to the waiting truck, and Schmidt said, "Climb in the rear seat with Neuhaus."

I asked him why they had machine guns with them. He said, "We aren't going to Christmas dinner. An adversary is just across the fence, and at a moment's notice, he could become our enemy." That thought sort of dimmed the lights on my mental Christmas tree as we rode down the mountain toward the border.

Nobody was saying a thing. I guess they were in deep concentration about the next four hours, being away from home on Christmas Eve, and the thoughts of what would be lurking on the other side of the fence once we got there.

It was beginning to snow quite hard as we arrived at the check point. I got out with the three guards and went into a tiny building nestled in a pine grove about 200 yards from the border. The windows were covered so light would not shine out and divulge the check point location though we all knew that the Russians and East Germans must have known where it was.

The guards being relieved hopped into the truck and left us there. Schmidt said, "I need to introduce you to Otto."

I asked who Otto was, and he said, "You will soon see."

Neuhaus went outside, and I could hear him talking. Soon, he came back through the door with a Rottweiler the size of a grizzly bear. I just sat there, looking at this monster beast dog, and the beast was staring back at me, not batting an eye. Schmidt broke the silence. He told me to call him over and to pat him slowly.

I asked, "What do I say? Does he understand English?"

Schmidt and the others laughed. He said, "Just tell him 'komme hier'!"

I said, "That sounds like 'come here' in English."

They all laughed, and Neuhaus said, "You're almost as smart as Otto. He knows Russian."

I didn't ask anything about that as I said "come here" to Otto. He walked toward me and stood with his nose just about even with my belt buckle. I slowly stretched out my hand and touched him lightly on the head. I watched his eyes slowly follow my hand as I put it on his head. I slowly rubbed the top of that massive head and began to massage one of his ears. He groaned a bit, and Schmidt said, "Good. He likes you."

I asked why Otto was there, and Schmidt told me, "He can hear, see, and smell better than us. These guns are only good if you can see your target, and, hopefully, there will be no targets tonight."

I thought to myself: me, too. I thought all the shooting was going on in Vietnam and Southeast Asia, but I guessed it was just waiting to happen right here if Moscow and Washington couldn't get along.

Schmidt said, "We better get going now. Tighten the neck of your parka. It's snowing quite hard, and the wind is up."

I stepped outside, and the wintry blast almost took my breath away. We split up. Neuhaus and Schonburg went to the left while Schmidt, Otto, and I took the right side. We were walking along, and I saw a signpost that read, "Deutsche Demokratische Republik." Beyond the post was the fence, about 25 yards away. I walked past the post and up to the fence and looked across into the little town that was nestled there in the mountains. There were few lights on in the town, and nobody was walking around over there. I said to Schmidt, "I wonder what it would be like to be in East Germany."

He laughed aloud and said, "You *are* in East Germany. That fence is not ours, and when you passed the post, you entered their country illegally. You better come back."

I got back faster than I got there. Schmidt was laughing to himself and said, "You Americans amaze me."

We walked along, and I asked Schmidt, "Do you ever see anyone on the other side of that fence?"

He said we had already passed two of their patrols. They stand still in the dark and let you walk by them unnoticed. The snow wasn't helping with the visibility at all tonight.

We continued our walk until we encountered two German Border Guards from the next outpost. I guessed this was their rendezvous and then they would head back to where they came from.

The other guards spoke only German with some broken English. One of them asked, "Christmas Eve, what do you do?"

I asked Schmidt to translate for me. I told them we usually sing Christmas carols and exchange gifts.

The German guard asked Schmidt something in German, and I really didn't know enough German at the time to try and figure out what he was saying. Schmidt said, "He wants you to sing him a Christmas carol."

I laughed and said, "Oh, sure!"

I saw the look on the German guard's face and wondered what song they all might know. Then, it hit me. They might know "Silent Night." I cleared my throat and started singing, "Silent night..."

All the guards suddenly joined in with "Stille Nacht...," the German version of the song.

I guess we all only knew the first verse of the song as we sang it three times before stopping. When we finished our joint choir, Schmidt suddenly whispered, "Quiet!" in English and German.

Through the wind and falling snow, I strained to hear what he was hearing. I saw Otto looking toward the fence. He was getting rigid as his ears perked up and listened. Off in the distance and drawing nearer was a group of men singing "Stille Nacht" in low voices. We waited as they drew nearer. When we could see their outlines clearly through the snow, one of them said, "Frohe Weihnachten," German for "Merry Christmas."

Schmidt returned the greeting. It was an East German Army patrol. They had heard us singing and had taken a chance on doing the same since the wind was howling and they most likely would not be heard by anyone who would turn them in. Schmidt and the East German officer spoke to each other in German. Schmidt looked at me and said, "They want to exchange presents. Do you have anything to give them?"

I used to smoke at the time, and I pulled out a brand new pack of Marlboro cigarettes. I gave them to Schmidt. He said, "Watch this!"

as he threw the pack of cigarettes over the two fences, which had to be at least 20 feet apart.

The East Germans went to where the cigarettes had landed, and you could hear them over there like a bunch of little kids as they divided the pack among themselves and quickly crushed the empty pack into a ball and threw it back into the area between the fences. Nobody would go in there because of the land mines.

The East Germans said something to Schmidt, and he told me to stand alone because the East Germans had something for me and I had to catch it. I said, "Sure." I was hoping it wasn't a hand grenade.

I saw one of the East Germans lob something into the air toward me. I never had to move. It came right at me. I caught it. It was a small bottle of peppermint schnapps. One of them had written, "Merry Christmas, friend" in English on the label of the bottle. I looked at it and said "Thank you" in English to the East Germans.

One of them said something to his comrades in German. Then, he said, "You are welcome" in broken English. We all waved at one another as we went our separate ways.

Schmidt said, "What are you going to do with the schnapps? It is contraband, you know."

I told him we had better get rid of it. So, we shared it with Neuhaus and Schonburg on our ride back to the barracks that cold, wintry night.

Many Christmas Eves have come and gone over the 43 years since. I often wonder if those East German guards got to walk where I was walking once the fences came down during the Reagan administration. I'm glad I was where I was on that snowy Christmas Eve in 1969 when the political fences came down for six people and a dog named Otto.

Hickory Hills Honey

If you were to be traveling about the back roads of South Carolina, you would see many a thing that would either catch your fancy or give you a memory you might well want to forget. This is such a story.

Leaving our hunt camp after a hard morning of hunting, our little group of trained killers set out in search of something to fill the groaning caverns of our bellies. We ventured into the little town of Clinton. Clinton was one of these small Southern towns that was going through reverse history, this meaning that most of the local industry had sold out to foreign investors and the mill barons had sought a cheaper line of labor outside the country rather than employing the local families that had brought them the prosperity and rich life styles they were so accustomed to living over the past century or two. Yes, Clinton was slowly ebbing away though a lot of the locals clung to the hope that the economy would soon change and things would return to what they thought was normal.

We drove through town and saw abandoned malls and companies that once were the heartbeat of the community. We were told that there was one little place that just wouldn't give up. The place was a barbecue joint, a hunter's dream, buffet and all. You really had to look for the place as it was located on a seldom traveled road off from the once busy highway that had been the main artery leading to and from the heart of town.

We found our turn and started down the little road that led to another little mill town. We hadn't gone very far when we found the place. Surrounded by a high chain-link fence was the gold mine where we had come to strike it rich. The sign out front read, "Hickory Hills Barbecue." We looked about and saw no hills anywhere on the landscape and figured that maybe at one time there may have been a hill on the site covered with hickory trees that had been carried away at some point in the name of progress.

We drove through the gate and parked our brawny pick-up alongside the trucks of the other hungry hunters. As we walked past the line of trucks toward the entrance, we did spot a pink Saturn, parked near the end of the lot. We wondered among ourselves who would be driving such an atrocious-looking vehicle, especially during the hunting season. We walked through the front door, looking for whom we thought the driver might be, but everyone looked the same.

During hunting season in South Carolina, just about everyone wears their camo clothing, no matter where they are going. You see, camo duds are a part of the local heritage, and beware lest you offend the locals by walking into their favorite eating spot, wearing sandals, sunglasses, a flowery shirt, and cutoffs. The beach look belongs down the road about 150 miles from here. I think you just might get stared out of the place if you didn't show up in the proper attire.

We walked past tables of hunters wearing their favorite brand of camouflage. The women and kids had on what they thought would hide them from the forest critters. I saw some patterns that hadn't been around in years. I guess these folks took care of what they had as getting more may have been a hard thing to do.

Everyone at the tables was gnawing on rib bones, drinking tea that had the consistency of honey, and merrily chatting away about what they had done for the past few hours before they left their hunting lairs to head into town for lunch. I watched them. They all acted like one big family. Maybe they were as this was a small Southern town. I was still looking for the driver of the pink Saturn.

We went through the line, loaded our plates, and then found a table by the back wall, which sported a large plywood cutout of a hog fanning himself as he sat on a chaise lounge over a small fire. I looked at it only once as it spoke for itself.

We were happily nibbling away when I spotted an old lady sitting in full camo. Her face looked like a deeply tanned, dried apple. Even the creases in her face had creases. She had on new camo gear and was wearing knee-high snake boots. I figured this was the owner of the pink Saturn and kept my eye on her, waiting for her to leave so I could see her get into the Saturn and confirm my suspicions.

I guess she caught me staring because she finished eating a rib, used two napkins to clean the dribbling grease from the crevices in her face, and headed my way. She came by the table and asked if I had seen anything that morning while hunting. I told her "no" as I looked at her. She kinda looked like one of the Li'l Abner characters: the old lady who smoked a pipe. This lady definitely did not smoke a pipe, though, as I saw what appeared to be the impression of a dip can in her front pocket. She must have known I was thinking something about her that I should not have because she bent over, gave me a quick kiss on the cheek, and walked away, saying, "There, dear, now you have something to remember me by."

The whole place was howling because of what she had done, and I was way too big to try to slide off the chair and crawl along the floor to find the exit while avoiding any type of eye contact with them. So, I just sat there until the laughter died down.

One of the patrons spoke up and told me I was a lucky man because "Old Inez," as she was called, had taken a hankering after me. I asked why she had singled me out for the kiss, and one of the kids blurted out, "Because she don't know you—yet."

The yet part had me getting a little antsy as I really didn't know what he was saying. He must have been speaking in the local code because the rest of the crowd was nodding in quiet agreement among themselves.

I caught a glimpse of Old Inez as she ambled through the parking lot. She was getting near the Saturn, and I was feeling good about myself, just knowing she was the owner, when suddenly she turned to the left and crawled up into the cab of a Ford F-350 that had a Hijacker rail system mounted underneath it and was wearing Super Swampers for rubber. She roared off down the road, squawking her tires as she shifted through the gears.

I stood there in amazement, not believing what had just taken place in the course of the last ten minutes. I saw this huge dude get up and walk my way as he headed for the register to pay for the herd of swine he had just consumed. I asked him what Old Inez's husband might say if he ever found out his woman had been messing around with an out-of-towner.

He said, "Don't hafta worry nothin' 'bout that. She is a widow. By the way, she is looking for a husband, and I think she has her eye on you." This brought on another thunderous round of laughter from the other patrons.

I had had enough. I told the guys we needed to head back to the woods. They knew why we were really leaving, and maybe the word *dear*, not *deer*, was part of it.

I paid the lady at the counter, who smiled with all four of her back teeth showing as she bade me farewell and welcomed me to come back again when I needed to "stuff my britches." I always considered my britches to be "well stuffed" because of my healthy size. A cruel thought entered my mind just then. Maybe she was talking about Old Inez and me! That was enough! "Let's get going," I said to the others as I walked out the door just in time to see the big dude trying to squeeze himself into the pink Saturn.

Lessons in Life

When a man approaches one of the final turns in life, he may look back down the path he has walked to see where he has been and if things could have been better if the right decisions had been made and if he really feels good about himself in this juncture of the journey. I haven't gotten to the point where I feel old yet although I am no longer a spring chicken. I guess I never was much of a spring chicken. I would call myself more of a hawk, always watching and trying to soar on the air currents of life.

This brings me to the point of reflection upon life. One day, while looking out my patio door window, I observed the kid next door as he was making an attempt to ride a skateboard down his driveway. When I say driveway, I should let you know the driveway is more of an asphalt trail, lined with pot holes and cracks, with a 45-degree pitch that catapults you out into the street. I watched as the kid made attempt after attempt to get down the hill without falling into one of the crevices he was so diligently trying to avoid. Time and again, he would start out, hit a hole or lose his balance, and crash to the ground. Crazy kid, I thought to myself. Hasn't he got anything better to do than try and end his young life on a skateboard in his driveway? I watched him for some time and saw he was determined to master the skateboard on a course most advanced boarders would avoid.

It finally dawned on me that this kid was different as I saw him starting out on a hard course when the smooth street was just at the end of the driveway. Unlike most people, who start on the easy slopes of life and work their way up to the intermediate, this little guy was tackling the hardest first and then working his way to the easy part.

The experienced part of me wanted to open the door and ask him why he wasn't starting out on the smooth road instead of trying to tackle Mt. Everest and the Grand Canyon at the same time, but curiosity got the best of me. I just sat back and watched as I was being taught a lesson in life that experience had somehow caused me to forget along the way. You see, most people will tell you that experience makes life go a lot easier at times because you learn to bypass the things that may seem mundane or not really that important. You walk by the garden and see the flowers but fail to stop and experience the fragrance of the blooms that are there for the taking. Here, watching the kid, I was going back to a time in my life when things were fresh and new and I didn't have experience to cloud the awe of a challenge.

There was something about this little guy that intrigued me, and I began to develop a friendship with him. Some folks may ask, "What do an older guy and a young kid have in common?" Well, actually nothing but the common desire to get through life, I guess, but I was learning to slow down and look at life through the eyes of a young person while applying a lesson learned to help point him in the right direction as he began his journey.

The kid and I talked quite a bit across the fence that separated our properties. The fence seemed to be a barrier at times, but neither of us looked at there being a barrier between us as we were using each other in our mutual learning process.

It really makes a difference to a young person when you ask him what he thinks about something rather than dragging experience out of your bag of life's lessons and beating him over the head with it. As we mature, we look at things differently, but we must never forget that we developed our life experience through a learning process that we abandon once the lesson has been learned, never looking back as we continue on our way. I found that by talking with the kid about life experiences I could go back to a time when life was simpler and the whole world was still before me rather than thinking of myself as being experienced enough to finish life on the trail of lessons learned. The flowers were there, but where was the fragrance of the awe of learning? I guess you could look at it like planting plastic flowers in your garden. They look nice, and that is all. Here is nothing that tells you they are alive and have something to contribute.

The blessed part about this relationship between the journeyman and the apprentice in this learning process is that the experience of the older is able to be transferred to the younger in a manner that the younger can process those experiences in a way he can fully understand without feeling as if he is "being told what to do." When I talk with the kid, I ask him about things in life to see how he feels and thinks about it. I remember back to the days when I was the kid's age and was going through the throes of life, but there was never anyone there to question or to listen to what my thoughts were.

South Carolina has Youth Hunt days, and I asked the kid if he would like to go with me on a turkey hunt. He jumped at the chance, and the plans were made. I think 100 or so e-mails and instant messages were exchanged in the weeks preceding the day the hunt was to take place. The younger was asking the older everything about what was going to take place that day and what he had to do to be successful in calling in and actually seeing and bagging a turkey. That was the normal exchange of information, but I toned everything down and presented it to him in a manner he would understand. I taught him how to hide in the brush and how to put the shotgun on his knee and remain still for over three minutes. For a teenager, that had to be an eternity. He had the courage to shoot my turkey gun, which is a Mossberg 835 3 ½ inch magnum ported out to a ten-gauge. It rocks me when I shoot it. I had the kid shoot it in the back yard, and it practically lifted his 102-pound body from the ground, yet he said he would pull the trigger again when the time came. Now, that inspired me! This little guy was going to experience some pain in order to finish what was needed to get the job done. I thought to myself that I don't know many older, experienced people who would do that. My respect for this little guy was growing by leaps and bounds, and the friendship was drawing closer as we were learning from one another.

Finally, after what seemed like months, though it was only two weeks, the big day arrived, and we set out on our wild adventure— the old guy with all the experience and the kid who was trying to learn faster than the experienced one could teach. We stopped by the gas station, and I asked the kid to climb up onto the truck and fuel my ATV. He gave me a strange look and said, "I never tried putting gas into one of these before."

I looked over at him and said, "Get your tail up there, and I will tell you how to do it!"

The kid hopped up onto the truck and took the cover off the ATV gas tank. I handed him the hose, and he looked at me with a look of "what now?"

I said, "Put the nozzle in the tank, and squeeze the handle. It will stop when it is full."

He did as I asked and soon had the tank topped off and the cover back on, had hopped back down off the truck, and was ready to go. The ride down to the hunting site was interrupted when we were directed to go to one of our other sites and help a new club member who was stranded in the woods with a broken-down ATV. We found him, remedied the problem, and were soon on our way again, discussing the set-up of the camp site and how we were going to spend the evening.

We finally got to our destination and began the tedious task of transporting all the gear down through the woods and swamp to where we would be spending the night. We were loaded to the hilt, and the road wasn't wanting to cooperate. Every mud hole was filled to the brim with water and had become deeper as someone had been there with a truck with mud tires, digging the holes deeper. I told the kid he needed to sit as close to me as he could so as to avoid a mud bath, and he tucked in so close that we must have looked like Siamese twins.

I came to one mud hole I knew was deep. Experience told me to go around it, which I did. I almost got stuck as the ground gave way and buried us to the axles, but we made it. We had to take two trips, and when I came upon the mud hole again, I thought back to the kid behind me, who was holding on the best he could and experiencing this ride for the first time. I remembered something as I approached the mud hole the second time. I used experience the first time and almost got stuck, and then I thought of the little guy behind me and the skateboard experience I had watched so many months back. I gunned the throttle and headed for the middle of this bottomless mud pit, much like the determined youth on the back had done when he tackled the driveway from the top instead of choosing the easy way.

"Hold on! Here we go!" I yelled to the kid.

I felt him draw close as he said, "Go for it!"

We cleared the hole with no problem. Lesson relearned from the kid: "go for it" although there may appear to be an easier way to do something.

We set up our camp site and sat outside until the middle of the evening. It was cold and breezy, and the kid and I sat in the field by our makeshift living quarters (turkey blind), looking out at the stars and all of the beacons on the horizon. The night was drifting by; the cold was getting colder; and the wind was getting windier. We decided to get into the turkey blind and get ready to tough out the night in the wilderness. I had brought along an air mattress, which turned out to be not as wide as I remembered. A friend had loaned me an inverter, which did not work, so I had to inflate the mattress with the two lungs God gave me. When I finally finished, which seemed like an eternity, I saw the kid smiling. I asked, "What are you laughing about?"

He said, "Are you light-headed?"

I replied, "No, kid, I was born this way."

I had the kid make up the bed. He put one of my poncho liners on the mattress and made a layer of blankets from his fleece blanket, another poncho liner, and a sleeping bag I had brought along.

The kid then introduced me to zombie movies on the DVD player he had brought. He told me when the movie started that he was going to have to fast-forward one of the scenes. I didn't question what he was going to fast-forward. Here we were—an old guy and a kid—camping on a hill in the middle of the woods far from any houses or other people, watching a zombie movie. I had never seen anything like this before. Here were these creatures biting people, ripping them to shreds, with blood everywhere. The people were head shooting the zombies to kill them. One zombie with no legs attacked a cop, and the cop was wrestling with the thing until he finally pumped lead into its head and killed it.

The kid looked over and said, "See that? No legs! Ha, ha!" This was a creepy film, and the kid was laughing!

He told me, "I have seen this thing a bunch of times."

That didn't allay my fears. Suppose some of those things were around here. I was letting myself be a kid again and was letting fear take over when I knew better, but I was doing it for the sake of the moment.

The kid said, "I have to fast-forward this part now," which he did.

I asked, "What was there? Something gory you didn't want me to see?"

"No," he said. "Naw, it was a girl who wasn't wearing much."

I was taken aback when he said that. I just looked at him. This kid was respecting me and wasn't making a big scene about it. Another lesson learned: kids don't have to be told about respect if you show them the same.

We were well into the zombie killing when I heard a noise outside the blind. It was only two inches from my face and only separated from us by the cloth of the blind. The kid stiffened and looked at me with wide eyes.

"What was that?" he asked. I told him it was a growl.

He said, "I thought it was a truck motor."

I told him there weren't any trucks out here, and that it must be a coyote. It was, and the critter was out there, going through our things. The kid wanted to take the 357, go out, and blast it. I told him to shoot for the head as it was probably a zombie coyote. He laughed. I didn't let him go outside right then. I didn't want to take a chance on him trying to wrestle a coyote.

He asked me, "What if the thing gets in here?"

I told him, "You let me take care of the critter. You just get out of here." Another lesson learned—this time from the old guy. The lesson was: the old guy is going to protect you because his experience in dealing with dangerous situations goes back a long way, and he isn't going to let anything or anyone hurt you as long as he can get between you and whatever may be attacking. There goes another point for the trust factor.

The critter took off after a while, but the next day, we found out from a coyote shooter that he had tracked a whole pack to where we had been camping. They were just on the other side of the logs beside where we had set up the blind. He said there was a pack of them there and that the coyote who came to us was a decoy sent to draw us out. I'm glad I made the right decision in keeping the kid close to me at that time. He did have to venture forth to the outside a few times that night as the bottles of Mountain Dew he was drinking were finding their way through his body, causing him to need to empty his bladder.

He did take the 357 with him when he went outside. The kid trusts the 357 as he is a dead shot with it, and he knows what it can do if he needs to use it. That is another trust factor I gave to him. I showed him how to shoot that pistol, and he listened well. I can actually say I am proud of his marksmanship, and I know that if my life were in jeopardy, he is capable of following through with using that pistol if he really needed to. Now, then, zombies, take that! The kid will get you with the 357 if you try to bite the fat guy.

The battery gave way on the DVD player halfway through *We Were Soldiers*. I told the kid we had about three hours until daylight, that the sun was going to rise soon, and that we had better get some sleep. I drew the blankets up around me. The wind was howling outside. The temperature was 39 degrees, but the heater was going. I was as warm as toast.

The kid rolled over on his back. I asked, "Are you going to cover up tonight?"

He answered, "No, l like to sleep on top of the blankets." When I am home, I do the same thing, but this wasn't home—and it was freezing outside.

I looked over at him and said, "Good night, killer."

I was sleeping away when all of a sudden I felt the kid kicking me and saying, "There is something walking around out there."

I was tired and remember telling him, "Okay, I will keep an eye on it for you," as I drifted off to sleep once again.

I woke up freezing about an hour later. All the blankets were at the foot of the blind, and I was covered only by the kid's fleece blanket. I reached over to pull the blanket closer when I felt something. What was that? I reached over again only to discover that the kid was under the blanket and was pushed up against me, trying to stay warm. Lesson learned. Kid takes advantage of old, sleeping man by stealing blanket from him. Old man gets kid to trust him, and then kid steals blankets and snuggles against old man to get body heat. Go figure! The heat ratio was wrong. The kid was getting four times the heat from me that I was getting from his skinny little self.

Morning finally came, and I saw the daylight fast approaching. I roused the kid and told him we needed to be on our way. I called, and a turkey responded. Only, I couldn't hear it. The kid heard it and pointed the way. We hopped onto the ATV and headed in the direction the turkey was calling from.

I stopped short, and we got off and snaked our way down the hill to where we thought the turkey was calling from. It called again, and we stopped and took cover. I called a few more times and looked over at the kid. There he was, with the shotgun propped up on his knee, waiting. Little "turkey slayer" alright! I was ever so proud when I saw him doing as I had instructed him days earlier. Moments like these make you feel good inside.

The turkey never showed itself although we had three answering at once during one calling session. I told the kid that we needed to head for the road. Once there, he told me he heard a turkey calling in the distance, so we waited, but it never materialized. We waited some more, and then we went back to the campsite, where we had sandwiches for lunch. The kid's mom calls him "the bottomless pit." I know why now. That's normal for a guy his age, though.

We then left and went to the river where I turned "Rambo Junior" loose with handguns and an SKS. I saw him put his ear plugs in before shooting. Lesson learned. He didn't question whether to wear them. I told him whenever we shoot, he has to wear them or not shoot. Self-discipline came into play here as the kid did what he knew was right without question. Atta boy, kid!

Nothing was safe from this little tiger. Cans in the river and the trees along the river were all targets. I was thinking to myself that the kid was probably imagining the trees as zombies and blasting away. Now and then, a gun would jam, and he would clear the action in a safe manner and proceed like a trained soldier. I just sat back and watched as his Airsoft shooting skills were being played out with real guns. Darn, this kid is good! I thought to myself as I watched him snipe trees and things floating by in the river.

All good things must come to a close, I guess. We slowly gathered our gear together as the sun began to kiss the western horizon. We got on the ATV and headed to the truck. We flew through the mud hole with ease and got to my truck. My son, Steven, was there with a friend of his. They were going to where we had come to snipe coyotes. Steven's friend, Brad, showed the kid his AR-15, which was fully decked as a sniper rifle. I watched as the kid took the rifle in his hands. He looked like he had just met Santa Claus in person. I'm glad he got to see a real sniper rifle and got to hold it in his hands. A dream come true for the kid! Lesson learned. That was a big deal for the kid. We older guys were used to shooting those things in the military, and it wasn't anything new to us. However, to see the kid holding the rifle and staring at it made me feel like I needed to appreciate the moment better, which I did.

The ride back was going well. We stopped at a Piggly Wiggly, and the kid ran in and got a bag of Snickers to munch on while we were driving. I told him not to eat too many of them as we were going to Hickory Hills to kill ourselves with barbecue. As we drove along, I saw the kid drift off to sleep. I felt good knowing I had been able to show him a great two days and that he was a perfect little gentleman while with me.

We pulled into the parking lot of the barbecue joint, and the kid came to. We went inside, and I told him to get what he wanted. He didn't heap his plate and didn't get a bunch of junk off the buffet. He ate what he had taken and then sat back for about 20 minutes. I think he was waiting for me to go get some more, but I had had my fill. He went and got a bowl of chocolate ice cream. A few minutes later, he got a couple more ribs and ate them, saying he was full.

When we were finished, we walked back out to the truck, and I told the kid he might want his pillow as the ride home was about two hours. He jumped into the back of the truck and got his pillow. While he was there, I told him he had better get a poncho liner to use as a blanket. He got both, got into the truck, and buckled himself in. He put his pillow against the door and pulled the poncho liner around himself. I wasn't five minutes down the road when he was fast asleep. I drove on through the darkness along the back roads I needed to use to get us home since the highway we normally used was shut down for construction. I would look over at the kid occasionally as he was soundly sleeping, and I was glad that he was there to share the night with me though he was asleep with no cares.

I had had a good time with the kid. We had grown to know and trust one another although there is a 46-year age difference, and I was thankful just that I had gotten to know him and was able to think of him as one of my own.

The miles passed, and he slept on. He never stirred along the road home. We finally got back home, and I had to shake him several times to rouse him from his sleep. He woke up and looked about as I parked in his driveway. I couldn't resist messing his hair up, and he didn't say a thing. He was now back home, and I had to give him back to Mom and Dad. The things I got from him and the things I gave him will probably never be forgotten. We are both better for the things we have taught each other. I am a willing teacher, and the kid is a willing learner. The same goes for the reverse. I guess all good things, such as this story, must come to a close, but this story will never end. This is just the beginning.

Addendum: I asked the kid what it was like to be 14. He replied, "Amazing." I ask myself what it is like to be fast approaching the age of 60, and I have to mimic my friend, the kid: "Amazing."

New Year's Eve Target

I was reading in an outdoor forum where a guy shot a moose with an arrow at about 12 yards. The problem was, the moose didn't drop in his tracks like the Nimrod had planned but looked directly at him and came at him at full charge. When I read about that hunter's brush with death, my memory faded back to an incident involving the mother-in-law and a moose. As I think about that moose charge, I remember how my mother-in-law came at me like that one New Year's Eve.

This was years ago when I used to imbibe. If you ever saw my mother-in-law, you would know why she reacted the way she did. Now, she was only about 5'2" and weighed about 390 pounds. If she were oriental, I would have called her Lo Phat, but she was of French Canadian descent (Canuck).

The guys were all on one side of the table, trying to empty the liquor bottles on the table. One of the brothers-in-law got the bright idea to set up the dart board and see who could throw the best set. The loser had to swallow down a half glass of the winners' choice. I'm no dart thrower, and I was losing quite a bit; being fueled by the liquor wasn't helping my aim any, either.

This went on for about an hour, and I was getting to the point of not seeing the dart board—or even the wall it was nailed on. I was standing—if you could call it that—and waiting my turn to lob a dart at the wall. I was holding the dart backwards in my hand and was just swinging my arm back and forth.

Suddenly, I heard this roar from behind me. It sounded like a wounded bull. I guess, when I was swinging my hand back and forth, the liquor running through my bloodstream relaxed me just a wee too much, and I had inadvertently let loose of the dart. It found a target. It must have looked like a torpedo charging toward an aircraft carrier the more I think about it. It seems that the mother-in-law was just across the room in a straight line from me. She was bent over the table, straightening up the snacks, when the dart caught her in the left butt cheek. It must have looked like a bull when a matador chucks one of those spears into it. Anyway, she let out this bellow that would have scared a cur dog off a gut cart. She was reaching behind to feel for what had impaled her. She had quite a girth and couldn't reach the dart. She charged around the room a few times. One of the women saw what was going on and grabbed hold of her while another pried the dart out of its target. The old lady was a-roaring about this time, demanding to know who her assailant was.

Now, everybody in the room was speaking French, and I wasn't understanding a word of what was going on except for some of the swear words the in-laws had taught me. I held myself up against the couch and tried to see across the room through the blur.

Everyone quit talking at once, and I saw the old lady looking my way. The women tried to grab her and hold her back.

"You," she screamed as she grabbed a butter knife off the table and waddled toward me. I understood the *you* but not the rest of what she was saying as she charged across the room toward me like a raging bull. I didn't have to understand French to figure out what she was saying was not very nice and that she was saying something about my imminent demise.

The brothers-in-law all scattered. I guess, they had seen her in a frenzied state before and were not taking any chances while the old lady was armed with a cutting/impaling device. I was trying to back up in my impaired state of mind while she charged and bellowed. It was like slow motion. I was trying to react without causing her to blow a gasket. I was doing a good job keeping away from her because I was a little faster on my feet. I was trying to hide in a corner of a round room.

I swear I saw her pawing the floor when she made a charge at me. I saw fire in her eyes as she got closer and closer. Nobody was making a move to help me. I guess, they had been victims of Mémé Vasche at one time.

I got to one side of the table, and she was on the other side. I was trying to hold myself up while at the same time to keep away from her.

I ran toward the wall, and I don't remember what happened next. From what I was told, the old lady came across the room, tripped over a rug, and landed on the table, which promptly split into two and covered her with the treats that had been sitting there, waiting to be consumed when the New Year's Eve ball came down the tower in New York City. Somebody got me out of the house and back to my place that night.

I saw the mother-in-law a few days later, and she didn't say anything. She handed me a box that had a new t-shirt in it. She told me to put it on. It had a bull's eye over my heart and another in the middle of my back. She told me I had to wear that shirt on New Year's Eve every year I came over to her house as she needed an aiming point for the new throwing knives she bought at the pawn shop.

I have since moved to South Carolina, and the dear mother-in-law is now roaming around the great pasture in the sky. I do miss her, but the idea of her being around sharp things is no longer something I have to worry about.

Rattler and Tiny

Rattler and Tiny were the two maintenance men who worked at a youth center where I was employed for several years. To see them would make you think back to some of the guys who chased Burt Reynolds through the woods in the movie, *Deliverance.* There wasn't much difference between them except these two hadn't been close to water for quite some time and, I might add, a bar of soap.

They were always quibbling about some little thing that didn't make sense to the rest of the world but was the main topic of their conversation for days at a time. One particular steamy day in July, they were deciding which jobs they were each going to do, and they were making sure one would not be outworking the other. I could hear them arguing about the heat and how they had to work outside while everyone else was inside in the air-conditioned office. They were kept outside as much as possible for the afore-mentioned reason.

Rattler took off in the company truck and said he had errands to run and things to pick up at the local hardware store. Now, this upset Tiny because he knew he would be working alone in the hot, July sun while his cohort was riding about town in an air-conditioned truck.

Tiny decided he was going to take it easy: hop on the lawn mower and cut the five acres of grass that surrounded the building. There was more red clay than grass, and Tiny was soon lost in a dust cloud as he merrily rode along on the mower. It was really hard to see the mower while he was on it. From the back, it looked as if he were sitting on four wheels and dust was coming out from underneath him.

He was out there for about four hours. He was sweating like a dead mule, and the red clay was caked on him from the dust the mower was throwing into the air. He almost looked made of brick. Tiny made one more pass and pulled up under a shade tree to drink a cold soda and to rest a bit.

About that time, Rattler came back and asked him what he was doing. I could hear them down there, yelling at each other. I heard Rattler ask Tiny what he had done while he was gone, and Tiny told him that while he was riding around in the air-conditioned truck, he had spent the last four hours baking what was left of his brains out in the scorching heat, cutting the grass. Rattler asked him if the grass looked good, and Tiny asked him why he had asked that. I almost fell out of my chair when I heard Rattler tell Tiny that he was going to have to cut the grass all over again. Tiny asked him why. Rattler told Tiny he was in town, getting the mower blades sharpened, and there were no mower blades on the mower. I'm really glad they didn't come to blows as they were down wind of us and that would have spoiled a perfect story.

Wally Amidon

The Deer with the Red Dress On

I saw him walking up the sidewalk heading to my office. He was a rather rotund, middle-aged, black man. What caught my attention was the white handkerchief he was waving about his face, wiping away perspiration as he ambled up the few steps to the lobby of our building and announced to the receptionist that he was from the Department of Mental Health and was here to see me. I got up from my chair, walked to the lobby, and introduced myself. I invited him into the office and offered him the larger of the two chairs arranged before my desk. He settled himself into the chair and commented that furniture makers were getting stingy these days because chairs were getting smaller. He arranged his coat and continued wiping his face although the room was air-conditioned.

He looked about as he introduced himself and spied a hunting magazine I had been looking through before his arrival. He spoke with a South Carolina low country accent that was hard for me to decode at first, but the longer I listened the more I was able to get an idea of what he was talking about. I don't want to lose the flavor of the conversation so I will attempt to transcribe the conversation to the best of my ability.

"Duz you hunt deyuh? Ah likes to git some now and den, but the Chief of Po-lice don't like goin' out affah dahk to find us night huntuhs. He keeps a wahnin us he gonna trow de book at us ifin' he catches us shinin' deyuh. But, you knows, he do de same thing wid his buddies."

I sat listening to him as he told his story. He reminded me of Louis Armstrong, using the handkerchief all the while telling the story.

He went on. "Let me tell you what happened to me and de old lady lass ye-uh. We live out in de boondocks in a trayluh. We got one wid four axles on it. You can't tell how many of the axles are dere because me and de old lady done covered de bottom of de trayluh wid aluminum sheets we got at de newspaypuh office. De problem stahted when dis big ol' buck deyuh come a-pokin' roun' de ol' lady's gahden. She planted de gahden beside de trayluh by de soybean field."

64

"What soybean field?" I asked.

"De soybean field de fahmuh planted 'roun' de trayhluh."

"You mean to tell me you have a trailer in the middle of a soybean field?" I asked.

"Sho' do. We lease de field to de fahmuh down de road. It helps pay de taxes."

I thought he was trying to pull my leg with this story, but he was dead serious. He continued, "Ah wuz out deyuh one mohnin', lookin' foh mah beans. Dey wuz deyuh when ah wints to bed, but in de mohnin', dey wuz gone, jus' like dat. Well, ah looks aroun', an' ah spots dis big ol' deeyuh at de oduh end of de trayluh. He got de biggest hoehns ah eber seed ona deeyuh. Well, ah stahts to hollerin' at dat deeyuh to git outta de gahden. Well, de old lady heyuhs all de fussin' goin' on outside de trayluh and comes out onna de poech, wearin' jus' de red nightgown ah gots her at de Dollah Sto' foh de anniversary las' month. She wuz a-hollerin' at me. She didn't have her teef in, so ah wuz havin' a hahd time unnahstandin' what she wuz a-tryin' to say to me. Mah name is Eustis, but when she ain't got her teef in, it sounds like she callin' me Uthliss.

Deyuh she is, a-stannin' on de poech in de red nightgown a-hollerin', 'Uthliss, git de deeyuh outta de gahden. Git de pitchfoek, an' a-run it through if it don't leave.'

Well, de deeyuh wuz a watchin' what ah wuz a-doin'. He didn't look like he cayuhd much foh de ol' lady becuz he had his eeyuhs way back an' wuz a-pawin' at de groun'. Ah wuz a-keepin' an eye on de deeyuh an' de ol' lady at de same time. Seems like mah eyes wuz tryin' to spread apaht de fuhthuh ah gots away from dem. Ah grabs de pitchfoek and heads foh de deeyuh. De deeyuh is pawin' at de groun' an' a-makin' deze funny noises like he et sumthin' an' a-wuz burpin'. De ol' lady is still a-hollerin', 'Run 'im through, Uthliss.' Ah wish foh once dat woman was hoahse becuza all de hollerin' goin' on.

De deeyuh seen dat pitchfoek ah had an' wuz fixin' to try an' run on me. He ran by me, an' ah stabzd 'im inna ham. Dat deeyuh hollid and come back foh moah. 'Stan yo' groun', Uthliss,' de ol' lady wuz a-hollerin'.

Ah wuz beginnin' to think that de deeyuh an' de ol' lady were in cahoots to git me. De deeyuh come by agin', but ah couldn't git a good stab at 'im. He run up to de poech an' snotted at de ol' lady. Ah really thunk he wanted to git dat red nightdress. Well, de deeyuh finally left, an' ah didn't see 'im foh a coupla days. De ol' lady thot ah wuz a hero foh a few days, an' ah wuzn't gonna let her down agin' if de deeyuh got back in de gahdin. Ah borrowed mah unkil's shotgun an' loaded it with birdshot. Ah tol' de ol' lady ah wuz gonna give de deeyuh lead pizzinin' if it dayud to show its face agin'.

A coupla days pass, an' de ol' lady woke me up a-hollerin'. 'Uthliss, git de gun, an' shoot de deeyuh. Look what its doin' out deyuh!'

Ah thot it wuz funny at first, but ah didn't wanna lose the hero status wid de ol' lady by laffin' out loud. See, she dun de washin' an' hung it out on de line to dry. Well, dat deeyuh spied dat red night-dress an' come an' tried to git at it while it wuz a-hangin' on de line. Ah don't think he thot de ol' lady wuz in it cuz de nightdress wuzn't hollerin' any. Well, de deeyuh dun got its hoehns all a-rapped up in dat nightdress and ripped it offin de clothesline. Ah guess de deeyuh couldn't see nuthin' cuz it wuz a-runnin' 'roun' in circles an' makin' dat burpin' noise agin.

'Don't jus' stan' deyuh, Uthliss! Git out deyuh, an' a-gits mah dress offa dat deeyuh!'

Well, ah snukked out de doah rell quick an' a-tried to git close to de deeyuh. Ah think he smelled me a-comin' cuz he snotted at me. He got de dress halfway off his hoens an' a-run off down through de soybeans. De ol' lady wuz a-stannin' on de poech an' a-hollerin' at de deeyuh to bring her dress on back an' foh me not to shoot de deeyuh cuz ah might put holes in de dress. Ah don't think de deeyuh heared her cuz he jus' a-kep' a-runnin'.

De nex' mohnin', ah wints to de gas station to gits some gas foh mah truck. Ah wints inside to pay up, an' ah heared dese guys a-tahkin' wid dis truckah. De truckah wuz tellin' 'em a stohry, an' dey wuz a-havin' a good ol' laff outta it. One of my buddies wiz a-laffin' so hahd ah thots he wuz gonna cry o' pee his brichis.

He seen me an' a-said, 'Hey, Eustis, come onna ova heyuh, an' a-heyah whats dis guy is a-tellin' us. Ah thinks he bin smokin' sumthin', but it's funny.'

Well, ah gits ova deyuh, an' de guy says, 'It's true. I really seen dis.'

Ah asked 'im what he dun seed, an' he said, 'Ah wuz a-drivin' down de innahstate a few minits ago, an' ah seen de darnis thing. Ah seen dis big ol' buck deeyuh standin' on de side of de road, an' you know what?'

'What?' Ah asks 'im.

He sez, 'Well, you ainta gonna believe this, but dat ol' deeyuh wuz a-wearin' sum kina redhoss dress. He had it in his hoehns, an' sum of it wuz down on his neck.'

Ah tol' de guys not to tell the ol' lady nuthin' 'bout dat deeyuh wearin' a red dress cuz it wuz a hers. Ah tol' 'em de stohry 'bout how de deeyuh dun stole de dress an' a-run off wid it. Dey all fell down a-laffin'. Dat soun's like a stohry, doan it?"

I just sat there mesmerized. Did I really hear this? Eustis began wiping his face again. I went out and brought him back an ice-cold drink.

He said, "Ya know, de ol' lady dun forgut 'bout dat red dress cuz when ah was ova in Colombia , ah stopped by de Walmaht an' a-got her two really pretty flowud ones." Eustis finished her drink and took care of the business he was there to transact.

I saw him leaving and went out into the lobby to say good-bye and to thank him for the story about the deer, the ol' lady, and the red dress. He said good-bye and was walking away when he suddenly looked back at me with a sly smile across his face, saying, "Ah sho' dat deeyuh doan like flowus."

Wally Amidon

The Hunkering Heckler

I used to sell ammunition at flea markets. I got all kinds of jerks coming by my table and yelling they could get ammunition for their rifles cheaper at Wallyworld and other third-world shopping centers. One guy in particular came around every week like clockwork and began his spiel when customers and other onlookers had gathered about my table to see what treasures from some far-flung corner of the earth I had brought them that week.

I had begun bringing Eliot, my old basset hound and close buddy, with me and chaining him under the table. Eliot was going blind, and he would growl and snap at things he didn't instantly recognize, especially if someone came up on him and surprised him.

The weekly do-no-gooder came by at his usual time one week and was telling everyone standing about that I was overpriced and that they could do better elsewhere. As he vomited out his barrage, he caught me staring at him. I motioned to him to draw near and told him in a low voice that I had something under the table that just might interest him. I told him if he wanted to see the hidden wares, all he had to do was lift the camouflage tablecloth a little, bend down a bit, and see what I was hiding from public view. He turned to the crowd and publicly proclaimed I had things hidden under my table and that they were probably illegal weapons and hand grenades. One of the onlookers began laughing and daring him to look under the table and see for himself what I was hiding. Not to be taken as a coward, the idiot bent over, lifted the cloth, and peered under the table. About that time, I gave old Eliot a nudge with my foot. He came to, only to see the guy's face about a foot from his. He bared his teeth, let out a loud growl, and lunged at his would-be assailant. I had Eliot short-chained to the table leg, and he almost pulled my table down the aisle, trying to get at the guy. The guy screamed and took off down the aisle, pushing people aside, and the onlookers laughed at what they had seen take place.

I didn't bring Eliot back after that incident. I didn't want him getting hurt or biting someone. The heckler would stop by now and then but would stand across the aisle in his supposed "safe zone." He would stare at the camouflage cloth, covering my table, and ask what I had under there.

I would say, "Guess!" Then, I would stretch my leg a little and nudge the cloth from the inside. He would leave without saying another word, thinking Eliot was still there. It was a little drastic, but everyone who was there to witness the heckler's run-in with old Eliot still smiles when remembering what took place there that day.

Wally Amidon

Part 3
Growing-up and (Maybe)
Grown-up Stories

Wally Amidon

.

Eben and Kate

Eben and Kate lived down the road from us. Down the road wasn't far enough for most of the neighbors who thought Eben and Kate should be living farther down the road than they were. Another state in another part of the country would have suited most of them. Problem with them was that they thought Eben and Kate were, well, as some would call it, undesirables in our neighborhood because they lived in a dilapidated house trailer that sat smack dab in the center of all the newer houses that had been built up around them in the ensuing years. The truth was that civilization had finally found Eben and Kate, and civilization was having a hard time dealing with their new-found neighbors.

If you were to drive by "the place," as Eben referred to it, you would think you were passing a county landfill. Eben never threw anything away because he figured everything could be worth something to someone some time. Between all the cars they had ever owned that were sitting on blocks and all the cans of junk scattered about the property, there was hardly any room for grass to grow, which suited them just fine as they wouldn't have cut it, anyway. They owned four or five lawn mowers, but none of them ever worked. They did keep the deck leading to the trailer cleaned off pretty good because they needed a place to keep all of their barbecue grills and cooking utensils. The deck was adorned with tiki torches, and the side of the trailer had those little, plastic, party lights strung along the side, coupled with the Christmas lights that stayed up year round. The tires of the trailer had succumbed to dry rot in the fifties, and Eben had never replaced them because he never planned to go anywhere.

Eben was a thin, little man, who shaved when he felt like it—and he never felt like it. He wore the same clothes most of the time and didn't really care what others thought of him because he and Kate were "here first." He would sit on his porch, drinking beer and tossing the empty cans into barrels stacked along the side of the trailer, when the weather permitted. The only time he ever left "the place" was when he would put his boat on the back of his truck and fish on the river for days at a time, leaving Kate by herself, which suited her just fine. Eben was a happy-go-lucky kind of guy, who only thought about drinking, fishing, collecting junk, and sleeping on the couch.

Kate must have been a looker a time back, but that must have been a long time ago. Her face had crevices within the crevices, and she kept her hair bleached and in a beehive hairdo. She was a sight to see at times, especially when she came into town to do the "tradin'" as she called it. She would drag Eben along, but he would usually stay in the truck and sleep while she shopped for the weekly groceries. They called this "getting along." Nobody ever recalled hearing them say something mean to each other, In fact, nobody in town remembers hearing them ever saying anything to each other.

Things went well for Eben and Kate. They really didn't have a care in the world. They didn't bother anybody, and nobody bothered them because of all the "Beware of Rabid Dog" signs Eben posted along the road as the neighborhood grew and started coming at them on all sides. The closest thing they had to a dog was a chain tied around a tree and a dog house Eben found at the dump one day. They never had a cat because the rats scared them off as soon as they came. Nothing ever invaded their little world until one fateful day when Eben had come back from one of his fishing trips loaded to the gills and fell asleep on the couch while watching his weekly wrestling show.

Kate had been outside, trying to clear a path though the "collection" to put up a new clothesline. She had seen Eben stagger from the truck and head into the trailer, having all he could do to get up the three steps onto the deck and through the door to get into the trailer. She didn't give his actions a second thought as this was his usual behavior.

She came in a few hours later and saw Eben curled up on the couch, snoring while the television blared away. She went over, shut the television off, and let Eben sleep it off. She went to bed that night and left him on the couch. It wasn't any use trying to rouse him just to tell him he had to go back to bed somewhere else in the house. Eben and Kate put their commonsense to use whenever they could.

Kate got up the next morning and walked out to the kitchen. Eben was still on the couch where she had left him the night before.

She called to him, and he didn't answer. She wanted him to go into town with her to do the shopping with her, but commonsense kicked in again. She thought she should leave best alone for the time being. Why wake him up just to get him into the truck so he could sleep while she was doing all the hard work?

Kate came back a few hours later, and old Eben was still curled up on the couch. She tried to get him up, but he wasn't moving. It seemed Eben had gone on another journey while Kate was in town, and he wasn't coming back from this one. Kate applied common-sense again, and this is where the story gets a little more interesting.

Kate loaded Eben onto the back of the truck and drove into town to the local funeral parlor. She drove around back and knocked on the door. Mortimer, the owner, came to the back door and asked how he could help her. Kate said, "Well, I was off in town shopping, and when I came back I found my man curled up on the couch, bent in half like a banana; he was dead. I brought him over here because I didn't think there was any sense of calling an ambulance or a doctor because he was already dead. They couldn't do anything more than what I am doing right now." Kaaa-ching! Commonsense kicking in again!

Mortimer was taken aback some but told Kate to come on inside. He would have some of his attendants (his brother and brother-in-law) bring Eben into the mortuary.

It was hard to put Eben onto a stretcher because he was still bent in half, and rigor mortis had set in pretty good. They waited till no-body was looking and then tossed Eben from the back of the truck up onto the loading dock and dragged him inside.

Meanwhile, Kate was working out the details with Mortimer. Kate, using her commonsense again, opted to have Eben cremated because that was the most economical (cheapest way out). She rea-soned within herself it would be a sin to buy a vault and a casket just to bury the casket in the ground. Besides, she could use the extra insurance money to spruce up "the place." Mortimer tried to talk her into buying a fancy urn, but she said Eben wouldn't have wanted any-thing fancy. She said she would bring her own container to put Eben in when the cremation was done. Mortimer thought that strange, but he was dealing with a strange lady so it really didn't seem strange to him when he thought it through.

A few days later, Kate showed up to pick up Eben's ashes. Mortimer asked her where her urn was, and she handed him a cigar box. She said, "Here. Put him in here. Whatever doesn't fit in here can be tossed out. As long as I get most of him, I won't have a problem."

Mortimer scooped Eben out of the oven and got most of him packed into the cigar box. There wasn't much left. So, he crammed it all into the box and put a piece of blue duct tape across the top to hold it shut. Kate took off with Eben and headed back to the house.

A couple of weeks later, Mortimer saw her in the supermarket and asked what she had done with Eben's ashes. She told him, "I got my brother, Herbert, to come on down from Gonic to help me lay Eben to rest. Eben liked to fish at the river so much I thought I would just go by and dump him in.

When we got there, a game warden was there, and he asked me what I had in the box. I told him I had Eben in the box and was going to put him in the river because he would have liked that. The game warden told me I couldn't do that because it was against some EPA law to put Eben in the river. I argued and told him there were a lot worse things in that river, but he said he would arrest me if I put Eben in there. Well, I didn't want a run-in with the law, so me and Herbert left. We waited until we thought the game warden was gone and started driving back toward the river.

Herbert came up with a brilliant idea. He told me to get up some speed and he would wait until we got in the middle of the bridge and then toss Eben and the box out the window and into the deepest part of the river where the swiftest current was, and Eben would be all over the place in no time. Well, I thought to myself, that is a good idea Herbert has. I told Herbert we would go for it. I got the truck going as fast as it would go before the front end started shaking and headed to the river. We were heading for the bridge, and Herbert had Eben and the box ready for the final plunge. Herbert cocked his arm back and was in the middle of the throw when the game warden jumped up on the side of the road and started hollering something.

I was going too fast to stop, and Herbert was past the point of no return with the throw. He let loose as we blew past the game warden.

I looked back just in time to see Eben and the cigar box slam into one of the bridge supports and bounce back into the road. A tractor trailer was right behind me, and it ran over Eben and the cigar box, scattering him all over the road. I stopped at the end of the bridge and watched as four or five more big rigs came along and ran over what was left of Eben."

Mortimer listened as Kate finished her story. He asked Kate if any of Eben ever got into the river. She said most of Eben was in the tires of the trucks heading south, and she thought it was nice that Eben finally got to leave the county and get out into the world.

Wally Amidon

A Joke Gone Wrong

When I was a kid, everyone would gather at the local check-in station, which at that time was the Mobile gas station, to see the deer that had been taken. The area game warden was there to oversee the check-in some days. One day, this guy from Massachusetts drove in with a goat strapped across his trunk with a deer tag attached to the thing's ear.

Now, you could tell by looking at this guy that he was not a seasoned hunter and must have come right off the main drag in downtown Boston. After all, he had on winter expedition clothing worn by the likes of those who were with Peary when he was on his way to the North Pole. His car was new, and there wasn't a trace of mud on the sidewalls of his tires—translated by us locals: he didn't drive the car off the road.

He got out of this car and began bragging about the nice buck he killed while the onlookers grinned and laughed to one another, knowing that in a few, short minutes the bragging would turn into a tale of woe. A few of the onlookers were heckling him with shouts of "Nice buck! Where did you get him?" "That is the nicest buck we have seen in here all year." One even had the brass tacks to say, "Hey, mister, you entered into our big buck contest?"

The visiting hunter was proud of all the comments being made about him and the creature he had tied to the trunk of his shiny, new car. Deep inside, though, he must have known something had to be dreadfully wrong.

The warden was watching this mini-circus take place and casually walked over and said, "Nice deer, mister. Only, here in New Hampshire we call that dead animal on your car a billy goat."

The warden walked to the back of the guy's car and inspected the goat. Then, he took out his ticket book and proceeded to write the guy a summons for shooting the goat.

The guy began laughing, thinking he had pulled one over on the warden. He pulled out a bill of sale and yelled loud enough for everyone to hear, "This was all a joke. I actually bought the goat from a farmer and shot it to give you locals a laugh about Massachusetts hunters."

The warden finished writing the ticket and gave it to the guy, saying to him, "The joke is on you, mister."

The guy asked, "Is it against the law to shoot a goat in New Hampshire?"

The warden was smiling and looking at the assembled crowd as he said, "No, but it is against the law to put a deer tag on anything but a deer in the state of New Hampshire. See you in court on Wednesday morning."

Moving On out of the Eastside

When you live in a small town, you get to know just about everybody who is anybody and some of the nobodies that nobody really wants to get to know. I grew up in a small town where people's status in the community was judged not by their actions and deeds but by what the local populace thought of them. It also mattered how close you lived to the river as to how high or low you were on the social totem pole.

In most towns in this great United States, riverfront property is held in high regard, and only the affluent can buy a small piece of God's Waterfront Kingdom while those with less than the lucky few who live within the water's reach have to live behind the affluence. Status dwindles the farther one gets from the river.

Now, in our little town, the reverse was true. The closer you lived to the river, the less you had and the less the townsfolk thought of you. You see, the mill houses were built close to the mills back when the mills were flourishing and the locals worked, sweat, and froze in order to make a meager existence for themselves and their families. As the mills died out, the houses owned by the mills were slowly degrading as those who lived in them were only renters, and the owners did not want to put money back into the slowly evolving hovels called home by many.

It is in this rugged section of town that the most prominent of the nobody families resided. It would be hard to list them by name as many of their relatives are still about and may see the names of their loved ones in print in a place other than the local court or police blotter and may just decide to get even with the writer of this story for elevating their social prominence without their knowledge.

There were four of these folks in this family who were known throughout the village as the least of the least in this nameless crowd who lived on the banks of the river. The elder was the husband and father of two of the other residents and was a brother to the remaining person. He was not a prominent-looking person. In fact, he looked as if time had left him behind and the present didn't care to acknowledge his presence. He was one of the folks who took a bath only if needed and *needed* wasn't a regular word in his vocabulary. He had the rough complexion of one who had worked hard most of his life, and he had when had hadn't been laid up in the bed drunk. He worked on the garbage truck, and everyone in town knew him by name.

If he had lived in the South, he would have been known as a good, ol' boy, but this was northern New England. People here never found any good in any of these ol' boys who were "below their social status." His name was Morton Priestly. The locals called him Priest although he didn't look like a priest or, as a matter of fact, like anything associated with a church. He wore the same clothes all the time, and people either recognized his face when they saw him coming from a distance or the odor he left as he walked by.

Priest never cared what others thought of him as he was his own man, and others' sneers or low talk as he walked by were kind of like music to his wax-laden ears. At least, people knew him by name and would talk about him at times. He was happy just to know that people knew him by name, odor, or reputation.

Priest went about his business without a care. Driving a garbage truck was high up on his list of desires. It was better than riding the back, especially when it was raining. He kept the loaders happy by giving them an occasional sip of whiskey from the flask he kept up under the seat of the garbage truck. You could always tell when they were nearing the end of their daily route as the truck was swerving toward both sides of the street and the loaders were struggling to keep up as Priest was listening to the radio, sipping his hooch, and forgetting to stop at times.

It was kind of comical to see one of the loaders get the garbage can up to dump into the truck about the time Priest took off, leaving garbage all over the street and the loaders yelling at him to stop while they assembled the mess and crammed it back into the cans the best they could to make a second attempt at dumping it into the truck and not losing any on the ground. They even made a game of it, yelling out consecutive dumping scores to each other and talking trash to each other—no pun intended there, folks. If you couldn't find your garbage can, all you had to do is walk up the street some and you would find it along the road or with the neighbors' cans because the loaders either got behind or Priest drove a little faster to get them to move a little faster and wear off some of the effects the whiskey was having on them as the day wore on.

One day, the people didn't see Priest at his usual station, driving the garbage truck. The local paper said he was found face down in the local landfill, clutching some faded plastic flowers that he supposedly found and was going to give to his wife. The paper had a big write-up about old Priest and his exploits as a public servant. The writer made him sound a lot better than he really was, and if he were around to have somebody read it to him, he might have agreed to most of it as long as it didn't make him look too good. The obituary in the local paper read that at the appointed time during the funeral service five seagulls flew the missing man formation over the landfill in honor of old Priest.

Humility was one of his traits. He never did anything wrong to anyone and always tried to be a friend to those who would let him get that close. He probably would have given you the shirt off his back if he had another to wear. The town would never be the same after he was gone. It wasn't fun to watch the garbage truck come and go any more. The town hired a sober man to drive it, and the loaders kept walking into the back of the truck during the route as they were not used to the truck waiting for them to catch up. The driver kept a jug of lemonade on the front seat, but the loaders would not touch it. They claimed it slowed them down.

Every now and then, I think back to many years ago when I was a young teen, sitting on our front porch and hearing the garbage truck, driven by old Priest, chugging up the hill. I can still hear the loaders yelling at him to slow down and the salty language they used when he pretended the motor was too loud to hear them yelling at him. To see him seated behind the wheel as if he were a king on his throne and the court jesters walking behind him makes me realize how simple life was for all of us so many years ago and that old Priest really was a king in his own right.

Rain, Fire, and Mad Cats

Living in the hills of New Hampshire can have its ups and downs. One of the ups was that neighbors were pretty far apart up on the mountain road where the wife and I lived. There are days when you don't have time to turn sideways, and there are other days when the weather can keep you inside and your mind begins to wonder into areas that should have "Keep Out" signs posted all around. Being a typical male, I was always open to some type of adventure as long as it didn't involve the local sheriff or the people who populated the junkyard on the other side of the mountain.

One rainy day, I got the sudden urge to shoot my muzzleloader. The wife wasn't home, so this was an opportune time to get in some range time from the comfort of the dining room. I put on some Johnny Cash records and proceeded to make a shooting bench on the kitchen table, using the wife's dish towels. The family cat was nervously pacing the floor and giving me the evil eye every now and then. I got out my black powder, bullets, and percussion caps. I poured the powder down the barrel and was getting ready to put a bullet into the muzzle of the muzzleloader when the phone rang.

I set the muzzleloader down on the table and went to answer the phone. I picked up the phone and said, "Hello." I was greeted by a female, calling about wanting to save the beavers in our area. I told the lady I really didn't care about her beavers and hung up the phone. Now, where was I? Oh, yeah: some powder down the barrel and load the bullet, put on the percussion cap, and voilà! I put the powder in, loaded the bullet, rammed it home with the ramrod, and pulled the hammer back.

The cat was peering at me from behind the wood stove. Its ears were laid back, and its eyes were narrow slits. It kind of gave me the creeps because it looked like a miniature panther, ready to pounce on some poor, unsuspecting creature that might be walking on its way to a waterhole.

I went over to the window and threw it open. Well, I didn't actually throw it open as the windows in our old farm house had the weights tied to them that kept them open when you "threw them open." A nice, modern, New England convenience from the 19th century! If you "threw them open" too hard, they stayed open, and you couldn't get them down.

The rain was coming down pretty good, and I was glad to be inside where it was warm and dry. I looked out to the field and saw I still had some targets standing up, left over from an earlier time of honing my marksman skills. I maneuvered around the table, set my rifle across the towels, and got where I could see the targets pretty good from the window. I pushed the curtains back some so I wouldn't shoot a hole through them. I didn't need the wife hollering about that. Besides that, she would never know anything about this indoor shooting range as she was shopping, and that was an all-day affair for her even if she had a short list.

I put the percussion cap onto the nipple of the rifle. I got good and comfy and was getting my sights onto the target. Johnny was singing "Ring of Fire." I was humming along with him and mentally noted that I would pull the trigger as soon as he broke into the chorus. I set the hair trigger and slowly touched the side of the trigger. The chorus was coming up, and I got my finger into position to pull the trigger. Here goes! Johnny started wailing, "I fell into a burning ring of fire." I touched the trigger off just as he said the word *fire*. Just then, a sudden gust of wind blew through the window, and the curtains fell back into place. I was past the point of no return with the hair trigger. The rifle roared to life and literally shook the house. I had accidentally double-charged the rifle with powder when the beaver lady had called and derailed my sensitive train of thought. I saw a huge fireball, and the room filled with dense smoke from the burning, black powder.

The blast, the fire from the burning, black powder, and the smoke literally scared the crap out of the cat, which was now exiting its lair behind the wood stove like a dragster leaving the starting line at the green light. The rifle had thrown me back from the brunt of being double-charged. I could hear Johnny singing, "I went down, down, down, and the flames went higher." Oh, no! The stinking curtains were ablaze from the muzzle blast. I tried to get back up, and when I did, the cat jumped on my back and tried to climb through the flaming curtains to get out the window. The cat was balled up in the curtains, trying to scratch its way clear and making weird noises. I tore the curtains down with the cat inside and threw the whole kit and kaboodle outside in the rain. The cat somehow got out of the smoldering curtains. I waited till the rain let up and then quickly hid them behind the barn. I lit up some foul-smelling incense to cover the smell of the gunpowder and the flaming curtains.

About that time, the wife drove up from her shopping adventure. She came into the house and asked what the rotten smell was. I blamed it on the incense. She then spotted cat crap on the wall and the missing curtains and demanded an answer. I told her the cat must have had distemper; it crapped all over the floor and the wall and got tangled in the curtains. She got over it and told me to shoot the cat again when I saw it in case it were rabid or had distemper. The cat never came back home. The wife did ask why I had ear plugs in as I had forgotten to take them out. I told her the cat screams were eerie, and I couldn't stand to listen to it "suffer." Glad I never got a second shot off.

Sharing Barney

There was a guy who lived up on the mountain by me when I lived in New Hampshire. He had a huge Saint Bernard, named Barney. That dog went everywhere with him and his son. The son grew up and moved off to college. The Saint Bernard eventually died, and the father left it at that.

The son came home with a group of his buddies one weekend, and they settled down to binging out in the barn. They were drinking everything in sight.

The father had a huge stew cooking in an iron pot over a fire in the back yard. Real rustic for the city slickers his son had brought along! The college kids took a break from drinking and went into the back yard—it was actually a large field—to have some of the stew the father had simmering away. The kids ate until they couldn't hold any more. They were gracious, though extremely drunk, and were offering compliments to the chef.

One of the kids said he had to puke and ran behind the barn. When he came back, he asked the father what kind of animal pelt was tacked to the barn drying. The son, knowing the family never kept livestock, ran to the back of the barn to see for himself. He came back, retching, and trying to tell his friends that they had just been eating Barney. The other guys thought he was full of crap and asked the father if what the son was saying was true.

The father didn't bat an eye and answered, "Ayuh. We don't waste nuthin' up here in the hills. A little protein won't kill you boys."

The kids jumped into their car and roared off down the mountain, leaving the father and son standing in a cloud of dust. The son looked at the dad and asked, "Was that really Barney?"

The father slowly walked away, then turned. He looked back at his son and said, "Well, it weren't Baby Bop!"

Smoking Cattle Herd

I was always an avid deer hunter in my younger years. I had only one problem, and that problem was having to learn on my own since I never had anyone to take me along and show me the finer points of stalking, finding, and, hopefully, helping to thin the local deer herd. I read all the books, listened to all the guys who brought the monstrous bucks into our local deer check-in station, and walked about in the woods in search of the elusive whitetail. I saw more signs of where they had been than where they presently were, but I never let those things discourage me nor otherwise dim the hope that one day I was going to meet up with Bambi's grandfather somewhere in a less traveled area in my mountain home of New Hampshire.

Some of my buddies were lucky in their pursuits early in life and gleefully showed off their trophies to those of us who still were waiting our turn to be the Daniel Boone in our small town. Years went by, and eventually I went into the Air Force, where I spent four years away from my home state and the local deer herd. When I returned, I remembered that my government had turned me into a trained killer, if you could call a radar technician a trained killer. I had shot holes in plenty of paper targets over the past four years during our annual rifle qualifying events, so I figured if I ever did see a live deer in the woods, I would have no problem hitting it.

Now I was home, out of uniform, and deer season was right around the corner. I found employment at Thompson Center Arms sanding and fitting rifle stocks for the Hawken, Renegade, and Seneca muzzle-loading rifles. I was able to buy a beautiful 50 caliber Hawken rifle through the company and learned how to be a pretty good shot with it. Learning to load, cock, and fire the rifle all in one fluid motion took some time to master as you had to have everything just right or you would have your hunt ruined by a rifle that would not fire when you pulled the trigger. I was all set to make my mark on the first deer I saw that season.

A few weeks before muzzleloader season opened, my brother and I were walking old, abandoned roads that led from our house, down through the woods, along the river, and then back toward the main road, looking for deer signs. We were coming up the old road that happened to end in the back side of old Johnny Wilson's pasture. As we came up on the pasture, we saw four deer standing among the cows, grazing on clover. We silently crept up as close as we dared to get a look at them. There were two yearlings, a large doe, and a monster eight-point mingling with the cows and filling their bellies on the sweet clover and other grasses that were growing there. We backed off and walked back down through the woods to our house, which was about two miles away.

I spoke of my plans to come back to the pasture on opening day of muzzleloader season and sneak up on the unsuspecting deer. I would come in from the main road after parking my car in the field across the road. I had it all planned out but had to wait one long agonizing day after another until season was finally open.

I had to work during the day season opened, but I took my gear with me and left after work to look for the deer my brother and I had seen earlier in the month. I found a good place to park my car in the field across the road and then began to assemble my gear. I loaded the muzzleloader with 100 grains of FFG powder and tapped the barrel a number of times to level the powder and also to make sure the powder had found its way to the breech of the rifle. I then chose a well-greased lead bullet and rammed it down on top of the powder charge. I carefully placed a cap on the nipple of the rifle and set the safety, which on that rifle consisted of pulling the hammer back to a half-cocked position. Every time I did this, I remembered the old phrase, "going off half-cocked" and now understood what that meant.

I worked my way across the road and walked silently down through the roads along an old stone wall that led to the pasture where I hoped the small deer herd would be, chewing away on what was left of the clover patch. I was passing through an old, abandoned apple orchard that was about halfway to my hoped-for rendezvous with the deer when I saw something that was going to drastically change my stalking plans and maybe have a detrimental effect on this longed-after hunt I was experiencing.

The cows were in the pasture, mingling with the deer as if they were family sharing lunch with one another. This put me in a predicament as I had to try and sneak out of the woods across the stone wall and try to blend in with the herd somehow. I was the size of some of the smaller ones, but the orange vest required by state law was something I couldn't hide. I then had a brilliant idea. Maybe I could sneak in from the west side of the pasture, and the cows would think I was the sun setting. That wasn't going to work. The wind was wrong. I crept over the stone wall, trying to be quiet and not loosen any more rocks than I needed to as I made my way into the pasture. Once over the wall, I hugged the wall and crawled a few feet at a time toward the herd, hoping the deer wouldn't see the orange mini-mountain coming in their direction and become alarmed and run off.

I was about 50 yards away and creeping toward the goal post (deer herd) when some of the cows spotted me and, being nosey as always, started my way, slowly plodding and stopping now and then to try and visualize what it was they were looking at. I tried hugging the ground as tightly as possible and turned my head away from them so as not to make eye contact with them. When I turned my head, I felt something wet on the side of my face. You guessed it. I was face down in a cow pie. It wasn't a bad-smelling one, but the idea I was face down in one made me wonder if hunting was worth it with all one has to go through. As always, trying to think on the bright side, I did know that one-half of my face was now digested-grass green, making my face invisible if I turned it right-side up toward the cows and deer.

The cows were finally standing around me, looking to see what I was. One of them decided she was going to sniff my ear and give me a lick on the side of the face. If you have ever been around cows, you know what was going to happen next. As soon as that mangy cow sniffed my ear, she blew backward through her nostrils, like a sneeze, nearly blowing my eardrum through my head. That did it! I wasn't going to lie there in the cow pie and take any abuse from a walking hamburger. I slowly eased up, put my hand on her back, and kept my head low.

Ol' Bossie thought she was going to help me get closer to the deer, I guess, because she was slowly walking a step at a time backward toward them, with me hugging her side and keeping low. We got within 30 yards, and she stopped. I peeked up over her back and saw the deer were working their way back to the woods on the side of the pasture. It was now or never, I said to myself, as I eased up, cocked the muzzleloader, and set the hair trigger, slowly aligning my sights on the buck that was with the group.

Things felt as if I were living in slow motion as soon as I set the hair trigger and took aim on that old buck. When the cow heard the double click of the trigger, she raised her head and turned back to see what I was doing on her spine. I guess she did not want to be there whenever what I was going to do was going to happen, and she took a step forward just as I touched off the round. Fire and smoke belched from the barrel of the muzzleloader, and the stampede was on.

Ol' Bossie and the rest of the cows took off running around in the smoke from the black powder, mooing and trying to get away from the place as fast as they could. They couldn't see where they were going because of the smoke and running into one another with me in the middle of all of it. One of them hit me sideways and knocked me to the ground. What a way to go, I thought to myself, as I hugged the ground and covered my face to protect it against the hooves that were thundering around me. They will find my mangled body in the middle of this cow pasture. I could just read the headlines in our local paper now:

Dairy Herd Kills Hunter in Stampede

Some people would even laugh at that, and my family would have to endure the talk that would ensue after I was gone.

All of a sudden, everything stopped. The cows were on the other side of the pasture and looking at me. I slowly stood up and realized as I pulled my face from the ground that both sides of my face were now covered with fresh, green, slimy cow pies.

I gathered my rifle and went looking for the deer I thought I had shot. Instead of the massive buck, I found a yearling lying where the buck had been standing. I also found a blood trail that left the pasture and went into the woods. I looked for an hour or so with no luck, went back, and put the deer tag on my prize. A yearling. My first deer. His size didn't matter as he was my first one, and I was proud of him.

I dragged him up through the field and to the gate by the road. Old Johnny Wilson came along the road and looked at my trophy. He said he had seen bigger, but they all tasted good. I guess that was his way of saying that my having a small deer was okay. As I was turning to leave, he said, "Ya know, I never seen anybody try to hide their face in cow crap before. Why don't you just use that camo face paint they sell at the Army Navy store?"

I didn't want to appear stupid or sound mean, so I told him, "Well, ya see, I like to go natural, and, besides, it also doubles as a cover scent."

I think he knew I was lying to him because as he walked away, he said, "Well, Sonny, you are in luck. I got fields and a barn full of that stuff you can have any time you want to use it."

I walked away happy and at the same time feeling stupid for walking around with cow crap on my face. I stopped by a brook on the way in to the check-in station to wash my face so I wouldn't have to go through another session of having to explain the purpose of the cow dung camouflage on my face.

I checked in my whopper. Nobody was there but the station attendant who checked in the deer. He didn't say a word until I went into the store and was paying for the drink I had bought to have on the way home. He kept looking at me kind of weird like, and I wondered what his problem was. As he handed me my change, he asked, "Mister, did you step in something?"

The next morning, old Johnny Wilson called me and told me he found a dead eight-point buck in his lower pasture and asked if I wanted it. I told him I wanted to see it and headed over to his farm. When I got there, the local game warden was there and was by the deer. He asked me if I had killed the buck, and I gave him my story of the cows, the stampede, and how I had gone looking for the deer. I told him I had never found a hole in the yearling and couldn't figure out what had killed it. The warden told me that Johnny could keep the deer and congratulated me for getting two with one shot although there were no wounds in the yearling.

I was about to walk away when old Johnny told the warden how I had cow dung all over my face when he saw me. "That explains everything," old Johnny told the warden. "That feller shot that buck, and the little one looked over to see where all the noise was coming from, saw that feller with dung on his face, and died laughing."

As they watched me slowly leave the barn and go to my car, they laughed away. Maybe I should have gone chicken hunting that day. At least, having egg on your face would have been better than what the locals were going to be told about what I had on my face that day.

The Hoss Bite

The writer of the book of *Proverbs* in the *Bible* speaks of a broken tooth and a foot out of joint. Now, just thinking about having one or another of those ailments brings the thought of pain to my mind. Either of those things would most likely have you writhing a bit and not having your mind where it should be. Pain is something I can understand and sometimes endure but not when it is purposely inflicted upon me. A foot out of joint or a broken tooth was used to describe having confidence in an unfaithful man in a time of trouble. I guess that really would hurt and get your attention right quick like. I am sure that if the writer of the book of *Proverbs* had lived another 3000 years or so, he would have had to list the "hoss bite" as another affliction that no person should ever have to endure.

I was introduced to the "hoss bite" at the tender age of 11 by my uncle, Alston Merrill, who lived in the woods across the river in Lebanon, Maine. My uncle even lived in a town with a biblical name, so I guess another affliction upon mankind would naturally come from a *Bible*-named town.

Uncle Alston worked all of his life. Whatever he did, he did to the fullest and would not stop until what he thought was perfection was reached. Now, all of this working and perfecting kind of turned him into a pre-Arnold Schwarzenegger type of strong man. He had a grip that was like a vise—no, I should say, more like a snapping turtle that wouldn't let go. He was a happy type of man, who always worked and took little time to relax, sit back, and look at what he had spent of his life building. It was always a blast to go to his house and spend a few weeks in the summer, helping cut wood, mow the lawns, and just find something to do to keep up with him when he got out of work at night. After supper every night, he would light up a Yankee cigar and head outside to work on some project he had going on. I loved to follow him about, getting a whiff of the pungent cigar smoke and trying to keep up with him and understand all of the information he was giving out concerning the project he was working on. I grew to love him and to trust him as he never said bad things to me in any type of way.

During the Thanksgiving season, we would all gather at his house for a scrumptious meal prepared by all the members of the family. Everyone was there this particular holiday. All the aunts, uncles, cousins, and my surviving grandparents were present.

The women were skittering around the kitchen, trying not to knock each other over or run into each other as they got their favorite dish ready for the feast soon to follow. The smells wafting from the kitchen were heavenly, foretelling a coming grand event.

The kids had all gone out to play. I was feeling like I was one of the men, so I lingered in the living room with my uncles and grandfather. I listened as they told of things that had taken place in our family from years past. I was all ears and knew my place: not interjecting anything into the conversation as it certainly would not fit into any of the subjects they were talking about.

Uncle Alston was telling the rest of those gathered there about the time his father gave him a "hoss bite." My interest was piqued, and I jumped into the conversation, without prior permission to do so, of course, and almost demanded of my uncle to explain what a "hoss bite" was. That was my first mistake.

My uncle rose from his chair and walked across the room, not taking his eyes off me as he drew nearer and nearer. The others started to smile and laugh the closer he got to me. I started to laugh, too, until he grabbed hold of my inner thigh with his massive hand and clamped down so tight I thought his fingers had gone clear through me.

This was just the beginning. He wouldn't let go but twisted his hand a bit from side to side. The whole room was awash in a roar of laughter as they saw the deer-in-the-headlights look on my face. My mouth was open, but nothing was able to come forth from it as the pain was taking its toll on my brain waves and the synapses were not connecting enough for me even to utter a groan, let alone a scream of terror. Now, my second mistake was uttering a string of expletives, aimed at my uncle, when I finally got my breath enough to say something.

My uncle was not a mean man. He never intentionally hurt anyone, but he was having fun with me that day. He finally let go. Everyone was laughing.

I was crying and ran out of the living room. The women were all wanting to know what was going on. I wouldn't answer them. I wouldn't go outside, either, because the younger kids would see me bawling my eyes out. I felt like I literally had had the inside of my leg ripped out.

I got back up from the chair I was sitting in and ran back into the living room to face my uncle. "If you ever do that to me again, you %^$#@!*, I'll, I'll. . . "

"What will you do?" my uncle asked.

"I'll give one back to you," I blurted out, with tears streaming down my face.

Everyone in the room started laughing. My uncle walked over and grabbed my shoulder. He said, "I was only playing with you. I wouldn't try to hurt you. If you think you want to give me a 'hoss bite,' you can go ahead and try."

I didn't make the attempt. I had called him a foul name in his own house in front of all the family, and he was apologizing to me! What a lesson learned!

For years, he laughed about this incident. Everyone in the family laughed about it. He even remembered the foul name I had called him that day and used to say he never heard a kid my age ever talk like that before. As I grew older, it bothered me that I would call the man who was mentoring me a bad name because he was playing with me. I talked with him about it one day a few years before his death. He laughed as he recounted the events and told me he had never thought badly of me for reacting the way I did. This cemented the bond I had had with him since I was a little boy staying at his house during the dog days of summer.

I last saw Uncle Alston a year before he passed away. I stopped by to visit him when we came up from South Carolina as he was now living alone since Aunt Alice had died a few years earlier. As we sat, talking about things of now and the past, he suddenly looked over at me and started laughing. I asked what he was laughing about, and he started on the story of the "hoss bite." He laughed until he almost cried. I knew he was thinking back to a happier time when my aunt, his dear wife, was at his side and working long hours to make their home ever so beautiful for them and others to enjoy.

He finished his story and asked how the grandkids were. I told him they were growing like weeds and that they all knew him by name even though they had never seen him.

"How's that?" he asked.

"Well," I said slowly, "they know what the 'hoss bite' is."

"You did that to them?" His eyes lit up, and he started laughing so hard I thought he would lose his breath. "How did you ever get that started with them?" he asked, tears streaming down the sides of his well-worn face.

"Well, I was telling them the story of my Uncle Alston who lived way up in Maine and how he gave me a 'hoss bite' one day. 'What's a 'hoss bite'?' they asked. You know what happened next. The family tradition wasn't going to be broken by me."

We laughed hard over this. As I was leaving, he gave me a hug and told me to be careful driving back to South Carolina. He had never hugged me before. Another rite of passage was taking place, this time about 45 years later. That was the last time I ever saw him alive. He had shrunk in size. Age had taken its toll on the body of my dear uncle but not on his spirit. That was still young and vibrant.

Now I am one of the old ones in the family. The grandkids come over and play and sometimes stay the night if they clamor enough.

I think back to the days when I was young and had no cares in the world, spending weeks at a time in Maine with my aunt and uncle, listening to the wind gently finding its way through the needles of the white pines that surrounded their house while drifting off to sleep in the depths of the night, and watching them build their dreams one day at a time while always having the time to share with others. It was kind of like living in a fairy tale in real life. The memories will never die. My sons and grandkids all know who my relatives are and were. They know just about everything, even the dreaded "hoss bite," which I am sure will continue on long after I am gone.

The Widow Steadman's Cat

Growing up in a small, mill town in New Hampshire has its advantages and disadvantages. One of the disadvantages is that the real world we read about and saw pictures of in magazines our parents subscribed to just seemed to be more than a day's walk from where we lived. Another disadvantage to small-town living was that everything we did in public was scrutinized by the elderly living among us and reported to our parents. We never got away with much with the aged eyes of the town acting as security and surveillance for the rest of the folks who lived there.

One of these aged reporters lived at the top of the hill on the street I lived on in my teenage years. Now, you see our town was laid out according to wealth. The more you had, the higher up the hill you lived. As chance would have it, we lived on the lowest street in the lowest part of town, but we didn't think any different as we didn't know any different unless that is, the people living along the way to the top gently reminded us of our physical address. We never much cared about living higher up on the hill because it was always hard to navigate the street when the road was slick with ice. During those times, the hill people used to ask my dad if they could park their fancy cars in our driveway while they walked up the hill in the cold. We thought it strange to have a house you couldn't get to in the winter since a quarter of our seasons were winter.

Now, getting back to the Widow Steadman. The Widow Steadman lived alone in her old Victorian house at the top of the hill. Her house was built like a castle. It had turrets on the corners of the front of the house. My dad said houses were built that way back in the Victorian era, but we kids swore she had it built so she could look down upon us to keep track of what we were doing.

We never saw very many people go up that way. The mailman would drop off her mail and would sometimes look back over his shoulder as if he were being watched. The milkman came early in the morning and left milk in the box out on her porch three times a week. Those were about the only people who ever had a reason to step onto her property.

The widow had a large, black cat that weighed about 20 pounds. That beast was her pride and joy. If you walked anywhere near her house, the cat would hiss and growl like a rabid panther, trying to make sure you didn't get too close. I guess, the cat was mean and old just like her owner as the local stray dogs didn't even venture close to it or bother to chase it.

It was getting close to Halloween, and all the kids in town were getting ready for candy, fun, and pranks on that scary night. Nobody ever went to the widow's house on Halloween because she would turn off all the lights in her house on that night, climb the staircase to the bedroom, position herself behind the curtains, and peek out the turret window to see what was going on in the town below. I think she thought we couldn't see her as we walked by, but the ominous shadow was there, betraying her hiding place.

Not many of us had ever seen her face-to-face and relied upon what we heard on the playground from others who claimed to have seen her. None of the descriptions were very kind and made her out to look like something between The Creature from the Black Lagoon and The Werewolf. Those descriptions made it even scarier to pass by her house on Halloween, thinking that she and her black beast would suddenly leap from the turret and snatch us away into the deep recesses of her cellar, which all the kids in town knew had to be a dungeon.

The wind was howling on this Halloween Eve. The trees made funny noises, and our minds wandered too far at times as we thought we saw horrid creatures peering out at us from the naked branches as we walked by.

All was going well that night until Homer Pickelsimer dared any of us to go and snatch the widow's cat when she let it out to patrol the perimeter of the house. Now, Homer was a kind fellow but never dared to do what he dared the rest of us to do. He promised the person who took on the mission his sack of booty, plundered from the neighbors, who would respond to a knock on the door as he went from house to house that night, filling his sack with all kinds of sugary treats.

Nobody wanted to get involved with the old widow in any way, let alone steal anything from her, especially the Satan Panther. We stood there, nobody wanting to be the first to say *no*. The wind was still howling, sounding more like the dead crying out as they walked the face of the earth on Halloween Eve, trying to connect their soul with a dead body. I think Herbie Peterson peed his pants. He told everyone he had to go home and check on his grandmother. We all knew Herbie's grandmother had died the previous summer, but nobody wanted to call him out on his desire not to be the first dead child hero in our small town.

Finally, one of the new kids in town, Johnny "Goofy" Mahaffey, agreed to perform the heinous deed. The rest of us were instantly relieved that we wouldn't have to bare our fears on that cold, windy night. Suddenly, Goofy found himself an instant hero among the costume-dressed ragbag army assembled on the street that night.

Homer told Goody he would stand watch when the cat came out and that he would give him an old mail sack to stuff the cat into. The deal was done. Homer and Goofy both spit into their right hands and sealed the deal with a spit shake. Don't ask me why we spit into our hands and then shook hands, mixing our spit. It may have been an unhealthy thing to do in the eyes of grownups, but it sure beat slitting our hands with a sharp knife and mixing our blood like our black-and-white television heroes were doing on the silver screen in those days.

The deal had been consummated and signed with spit, and we all watched Homer and Goofy slowly walk up the hill toward the Widow Steadman's house. Our little group followed as supporters but at least 100 yards back just in case things got out of hand and we needed a head start to run back down the street. It seemed like an eternity just to walk up the street, walking toward an uncertain experience that was soon to transpire. I guess it seemed like time without end as none of us were skipping up the hill, knowing that the widow might snatch one of us to keep her in her dungeon until she could decide upon a horrible fate for her captive.

Finally, Homer and Goofy reached the widow's house and took their places behind the rock wall that separated the house from the street. Homer was to keep a watch on the turret to see if and when the shadow moved from the sniper perch. He would signal Goofy when and if the shadow moved away from the window as that might be when the widow would let the cat out. It seemed like ages passed before the signal was sent.

Goofy moved in with the sack provided by Homer. He bent over and crawled up through the shrubs in the front yard to get as close to the house as he dared. Homer kept watch behind the house and had earlier agreed to make a cat call if he spotted the widow outside the house, hoping the widow would think her cat had a friend waiting for it outside the house.

Goofy waited for about five minutes when he saw a black shape drawing near. He backed up against the house foundation with the open sack spread before him, waiting for the prey to get closer. No signal from Homer yet, so the coast must be clear!

The shape drew nearer and paused just as Goofy made one fell swoop and gathered the quarry into the sack. "Gotcha, Satan cat!" he said as he drew the drawstring on the sack as tight as he could while the critter inside was desperately clawing the inside of the bag, vainly trying to escape the cloth prison it suddenly found itself in.

Goofy crawled across the lawn and made it to the wall where he found Homer. "What ya got in the bag, Goofy?" he whispered just in case something was lurking near the wall.

"I got the old widow's cat in here. Let's get out of here before she finds out what we did."

Homer said, "Man, that was quick! I didn't see her even move from the window. You are right. We better get out of here."

They ran back down the street, and the rest of us followed the heroes back to where the deal had taken place. Goofy came up with an intelligent question. "What are we going to do with the cat now that we have it?"

Nobody had an instant answer. So, we left the sack in my dad's garage while we finished our evening of trick-or-treating.

We decided to quit when it became a burden to carry the heavily laden candy sacks up and down the street and elected to go to my house and check out our booty. Homer told Goofy to get the sacked cat. We would bring it into the living room, surround it in a circle, and taunt it a bit before turning it loose to run back up the hill to its master. That would teach the mean old cat. It wouldn't mess with us anymore after we finished with it.

We got to my house, went to the living room, and checked the contents of our candy sacks. We rummaged through our goodies and traded off the things we didn't really like. There was a small pile of apples sitting by itself on the rug as none of us thought apples had any trading value, and, besides that, they didn't fit into a kid's food pyramid.

Alice, the girl with the buck teeth and freckles, noticed the cat bag stirring. She suggested we put the bag in the circle and let the cat out. Since Goofy had caught it, he was elected to let it out. He fought with the drawstring before it finally gave way. The creature inside must have seen a speck of light and decided to propel itself from captivity. Goofy held the bag up to his face and was peering into it when the creature rocketed out of the bag, propelled itself off from Goofy's shoulder, and began to run across the living room floor toward the kitchen where my mom was washing the dishes and my dad was sipping a cup of coffee. I stared in horror as I watched the creature draw closer to the kitchen.

"Goofy!" Homer screamed. "The widow's cat is jet black and doesn't have two white stripes on its back."

"Skunk!" Homer screamed as he dove behind the couch, and the rest of us sought refuge in closets and behind furniture. I knew the widow never moved from the window, Homer thought to himself.

Meanwhile, my dad heard the commotion going on in the living room and was getting up from the table when the skunk made its entrance. "What the blank is that thing doing in my house?" he hollered just as I heard my mother's scream, the breaking of glass, a table turning over, and chairs being thrown.

Suddenly, my nostrils were filled with the horrid odor of skunk essence, and the commotion, my dad's ranting, and my mother's screams grew louder. The skunk ran from the kitchen and made a beeline for the back of the couch where Homer was hiding. I don't know who scared the other the most, but the skunk certainly left its mark on Homer, who jumped over the couch and ran out the front door, leaving a trail of his newfound scent behind him.

The skunk saw the open door and followed Homer outside. Needless to say, the rest of the kids scattered to any open exit to escape the carnage and ran home to a more secure environment.

My dad emerged from the kitchen with a large butcher knife in his hand, looking to murder the creature that had caused such mayhem in his little sanctuary. I looked up at him and didn't dare to say a word as I made my way to my bedroom.

The house was totally wrecked. The kitchen looked like a battle zone—my dad and the skunk had made Custer's last stand look like a picnic. The living room was covered with candy, scattered by the former owners as they had fled the scene. The house was filled with the pungent odor of the skunk. It was beginning to make my eyes water though I was down the hall behind the bedroom door.

I heard the doorbell ring, followed by my father's heavy footsteps treading across the living room to answer the front door. It was the last of the trick-or-treaters, who were making a late-night visit to gather any remnants of candy that might be left in the neighborhood.

My father answered the door. Three kids between the ages of 9 and 12 stood there, festooned in their costumes. They didn't have a chance to say, "Trick or treat" before my dad said, "Trick!" A blast of skunk scent wafted through the door and attacked their young, unsuspecting nostrils.

The kids had seen all the candy scattered on the floor, but once the skunk scent hit them, they made a hasty retreat. I heard them talking among themselves as they quickly walked down the sidewalk and headed back up the hill to their homes. "Did you see all the candy that dude had on his floor? Man, those poor people must live on the stuff."

Just as they were getting out of earshot, I heard the older one say, "Yeah, all that candy, and the dude doesn't have enough money to buy a bar of soap!"

Part 4
Observations on Life

Wally Amidon

Bobblehead Babtist Church/Being Filled

I purposely misspelled the word, *Baptist,* in the title of this little story because most of what I am going to write about comes from the region of the country where people refer to themselves as "Babt-pist," that is, as if they separating themselves from the rest of the Baptists in this great country of ours.

I go to church on a regular basis myself, and when I travel, I try to find a local congregation that will make me feel as I am one of them. Most of them do, and the others don't quite know what they are missing out on. One day, they will see the fallacy of their not wanting to rush up, introduce themselves to me, and try to help me fit in with them for the short time I will be with them.

I like to watch people from the corner of my eye and keep an eye on the preacher at the same time, just in case he may happen to look my way and see me staring off in another direction. It really doesn't make you popular with the preacher if you are visiting and looking about at his congregation as if you were sizing them up for some future event.

When sitting in the church auditorium, I like to sit somewhere near the middle. The back seats are all usually taken by the regulars, who like to attend but like to keep their distance just in case the preacher makes a comment that may have an impact upon their conscience and show on their face. The front rows are usually taken by those who don't hear well, want to show their support for their local preacher, or just plain walk in late.

Now, the bobbleheads usually sit just shy of the middle but heading to the back. What is a bobblehead you may be asking yourself. A bobblehead is the person who constantly nods his head in animated approval of what the preacher may be saying at the moment. Bobble heads come in a few categories, and I will try to describe them the way I have observed them over the past 30 years.

Categories of Bobble Heads

The Super Bobblehead

This person is constantly nodding his head up and down. Sometimes, he is nodding his head up and down with his eyes closed as if he is in deep concentration, trying to wring every word out of what is being said as if his very life depended upon it. I have actually heard some super bobbleheads get their minds so entwined with what is being spoken that they actually reply with a holy snore. Others keep their eyes wide open and on the preacher although their heads are bouncing up and down as if they were connected with springs and they were driving down a bumpy back road out in the country. These folks amaze me with their eye contact. They are like an Abram's tank; the barrel stays in one place although the rest of the tank may be climbing or descending a hill. I guess they think the nodding of their heads and the constant eye contact make the preacher feel good. Kind of zombie-like, if you ask me. They are good folks, just trying to look attentive and be in the good graces of the other bobbleheads who may be sitting near them. I should note that the bobbleheads only nod in church. You will never see them out in public being a bobblehead. Someone might just think they were a "Babtist."

The Semi-Bobblehead

This person will occasionally nod his head in agreement as if he is discerning what is being said. He nods at about half the speed of the super bobblehead. A good point is that this person is not distracting. His movements are like a semi-automatic rifle. The bobbles may occur when certain phrases are being spoken or when the pitch or tone of the preacher's voice changes. This person is showing discerning approval with a contented look upon his face. At times, he will even blink or look around.

Disconnected Bobblehead

This person will nod his head at specific intervals. He will hold his head by grasping his chin in his right hand and placing his forefinger across his lips as though he is trying to block any lip movement that may be interpreted by others as a hostile or impolite reaction to what is being spoken in the pulpit.

Verbal Bobbleheads

If you are in a lively church, you will have those sitting around you, saying "Amen" to every other word the preacher speaks even though he may have just said, "People are dying and going to hell this very moment." I refer to these folks as verbal bobbleheads.

Other Bobbleheads

We have discussed a few types of bobbleheads, but we can't let a sampling of some of the others go without mention.

If you scrutinize the crowd, you may see one or two people taking notes. If you look closely, you may find that one of these people is trying to balance his checkbook which is opened between the pages of his *Bible*.

Then, you have the pew artist. This person will draw caricatures of others in the congregation and sometimes of the preacher and then pass the picture to the person sitting beside him to get his reaction. If that person laughs, the preacher will wonder what he said that was so funny.

Of course, we can't let the text message person go. He will text message someone outside the church, making plans for the afternoon or making comments about some of the people sitting near him.

We can't forget the runners, either. These folks will actually get up, run around the aisle like a NASCAR vehicle going full throttle, yelling and screaming as if a wildcat were tearing them limb from limb, and then will jump over a pew or two to get back to the starting line. At times, P. T. Barnum would have been jealous of the acts he might see going on in a church.

Encounter

Now, I have seen some stranger things, and I will make a feeble attempt to capture the spirit of one of these encounters in the following story:

Once, I was driving along a back road up in the mountains of Tennessee just after sunset. It was raining; the darkness was thick; and my headlights were fighting to penetrate the black curtain I was attempting to drive through. I drove around hairpin turns so tight I could literally (well, almost) see my license plate in the rearview mirror. No towns were in sight, and I didn't see any road signs. As I drove along, I wondered if there were any people living about this part of the wilderness. I came around the corner and saw the lights of a small building. There were a few pickup trucks parked out front, and I saw a horse standing under a shed. As I got closer, I could see a hand-painted sign on the side of the building which read:

BROKE HEART BAPTIST CHURCH
MEETING TIME: AFTER DARK
ELIJAH DANDYBANKS, PREACHER

This sign piqued my interested, so I decided to take a break and walk in. Maybe I just might be able to spot a few new categories of bobbleheads to add to my list. I slowly opened the back door so as not to make a lot of racket coming in. The preacher was a-ripping a sermon but stopped in mid-sentence when he saw my half-drowned figure enter the front door. "Welcome, my brother," he said with a smile. "Take your coat off and join us for a spell; we are just getting started."

Then, he returned to finish the sentence he had started when I walked in. It was like a CD being paused and then started again. Clearly, nobody thought that was a little strange but me as they were all hollering, "Amen, Brother! Preach it!" I didn't want to feel out of place so I started doing as the others and hollering, "Amen, Brother," throwing my hands into the air and letting out a holy holler or two if others around me were doing the same.

About 15 minutes into the sermon, I was beginning to work up a sweat. The old lady sitting beside me was constantly wiping her mouth with a rag. I was wondering what she was wiping as I couldn't really see her mouth that well. She saw my sweaty face and turned toward me. When she smiled, I didn't see any teeth. She had been gumming the rag to control her shouting. She took the rag, snapped it open, and before I could get my hands up, began wiping the perspiration from my face.

I threw my hands into the air and tried to get the rag out of my face. The rest of the congregation must have thought I was getting into the spirit as they all rose to their feet and began clapping their hands. The old lady had a grip on the back of my neck, and I was trying to push her hands away, but to no avail. I reached into the air to grab the rag from her grip. I missed. I opened my hand to get another try at the rag when I felt something cold moving in my hand. I thought I had finally gotten hold of the wet, slimy rag, but I could see that the old lady still had it and was now backing away a bit and joining in the clapping of hands with the rest of the congregation.

I looked to see what had been handed to me, and, to my horror, I saw I was holding a timber rattler about two feet long. It was swaying to the clapping, and now the members of the congregation were working themselves into a frenzy. I heard one man say, "An apostle has been sent our way. Praise the Lord!"

I didn't want to throw the snake into the crowd for fear it might bite someone. The snake wasn't trying to coil. I thought maybe this was an old rattler with no fangs until it drew near to my face and opened its mouth to bare two white fangs about three inches from my nose. I lifted the snake into the air as high as I possible could, thinking if it did strike, it could only get my forearm.

I saw an old man staring at me with tears in his eyes. Maybe he wants the snake, I thought to myself and inched my way toward him. I tried to hand him the snake but saw he was missing an arm and his left hand was withered. No help here.

Finally, a white-haired fellow took the snake from my hands and began walking with it above his head. The congregation was going wild. The pianist was playing *I'll Fly Away*, and I wished at that time I was a bird and could have done the same. People were drawing around me and complimenting me on my "faith." Strange word for terror, but I didn't let on. I found a seat near the middle of the church and quickly sat down as I saw the snake wasn't being handled by anyone sitting down.

The rag lady was heading toward me, and I quickly covered my face to prevent a second dose of face washing. She passed by me. My prayer had been answered for the moment.

I guess the faith part of the service was over. They retired the timber rattler to his box. A man with a banjo walked to the podium and began strumming *Only Trust Him* as the congregation began to join in singing the words. I looked about but didn't see any hymn books. I asked the man beside me where the hymn books were as I didn't know all the words. He replied, "Ain't got any. Nobody here can read, anyway. We just grew up singing these songs."

In the back of mind, I knew they would never sing Handel's *Messiah*. The singing went on for another 20 minutes or so.

The preacher returned to the podium and asked that the congregation please pray for the One God had sent to them that cold, rainy evening. I was halfway wondering who the "One" was when it dawned on me I was the One. The prayer ended, and all the people came to say good-bye. Not wanting to be un-Onely, I thanked them for letting me join with them and experience my strong faith with them.

Finally, the last person shook my hand, and I walked to the door. The preacher was standing there. He looked me up and down and said, "I sense you have been filled in more ways than one tonight. There's an outhouse out back if you care to clean yourself up a bit. No running water or the sorts but plenty of clean cobs. Come back and see us again."

I didn't bother going to the outhouse. I went to my car, climbed in, and began driving down the road. The rain had let up some, and I could see a little better as I drove on. I was happy being in the security of my nice, warm car once again and knowing I had a roll of paper towels in the trunk to use to clean myself up once I found a gas station.

Things I Learned in the School of Hard Knocks

So, I am going to take a break from storytelling for a bit in order to share some important things that these stories—and the life that found itself in the middle of these stories—have taught me. Here they are:

1. Always be true to your friends and family. They depend upon you for support at times, and you may be the person who shatters their world.

2. Never lie, deceive, or otherwise be untruthful to your friends and family. They expect you to be truthful with them.

3. If you get mad and unload on friends, always remember that if they are really true friends, they will understand you are just having a bad day and will not hold it against you even if it takes years for you to apologize for what you have done to them.

4. Never take advantage of other people. It will come back to haunt you as they know what you are doing although they may not let you know at the moment.

5. Apologize when you are wrong. It takes a man to admit when he is wrong.

6. Look people in the eye when you talk with them.

7. If you are right, never back down.

8. Be a gentleman around females. Never let urges ruin your future.

9. Think before acting. How will what I do today affect me tomorrow?

10. Listen to your parents although you may disagree with them. They love you, and that is why they are hard on you at times. If they did not love you, they would let you run wild.

11. Remember, your tongue can be like a shotgun. You may shoot it off, but you can't get back the words you shot the other person with. Your wounds really hurt them.

12. If your heart is hurting, tell someone. Holding it in only hurts worse.

13. Tell your family you love them. They need to hear it vocalized. Never think they take it for granted. Give them a hug and really mean it.

14. Write to your friends and let them know how you really feel about them. It will mean a lot to them, and they will re-read your note when times are rough for them. They will know they have a real friend somewhere out there.

15. Care about the little things in life. Little things add up to bigger things.

16. Never let past experience be your ultimate guide. Stop and look at the situation. You may learn something new from it.

17. Remember, kids are only little humans who feel just like you do. Never look down on them or think they are stupid just because they don't know everything you do right now. You can learn a lot from younger people if you give them the chance.

18. Treat everyone as you would like for them to treat you.

19. A friend can be closer than a brother at times, but your brother is your brother forever.

20. Always look at other people in a positive way although you may not want to.

21. Be true to yourself. Others may not be so kind.

22. Your trust in your friends and family will always be tested, sometimes by others. Remember that a developed trust is solid like a rock, no matter what may be happening at the time.

23. Whatever you set out to do, finish it. The world is full of people who wish they would have done what their heart told them to do years earlier.

24. Remember that you are a human being, who needs love, trust, and support from your friends and family. You can't go through life on your own. You are not as tough as you think you are.

25. Try to make life a little easier and brighter for the people who are around you. Some may try to take advantage of your kindness toward them, but that should never stop you from doing good unto others.

26. Be thankful for who you are, what you have, and the people who love and care for you. Those are the things in life that will make you a better human being.

One day you will be somebody's parent. Will you be able to pass any of this on to your children? I learned all of this on my own because I never had anyone who had the time to teach me these things, but I care enough about you to share with you what I have learned so far in my life.

Making Life Easier and Brighter

One Christmas season when we were at Walmart here in Travelers Rest, we had a basket full of anything you can think of. The line was long. Many people had full baskets. Finally, we got to the register.

As I turned to empty the cart, I saw this young black man standing in line with a carton of orange juice and a can of soda. He looked at me and smiled. I told him to go ahead of us since he had only two things to buy. He thanked me and paid for his things.

As he was leaving, he turned to us and said, "Thank you again."

I shook hands with him. "Merry Christmas," I wished him. He smiled and said thank you.

Another family was standing behind us. They had a couple of little kids with them who were chattering away with excitement—and were pushing two baskets brimming to the top. The father was wearing a Boiling Springs Fire Department coat. He looked over at me and said, "Thank you."

"What for?" I asked him.

"For letting that man ahead of you go through the line without having to wait for you to unload all of your things," he said.

"I have learned by example over the years," I told him. "I was just passing it on."

He smiled. "I am seeing less and less of good will toward others these days," he commented.

"Well," I replied, "that shouldn't stop the rest of us from doing good."

"You are right about that," he said.

We had to leave right about then. As we were leaving, I heard one of the kids say, "That guy looks like Santa Claus."

"Shh!" said the mom. "Be quiet, and quit saying things like that about people."

The dad turned toward the little girl. "It's ok," he said. "Maybe he really was Santa Claus."

I laughed inside for a few minutes. Oh, the things we can do when we just stop and put others first in our hectic lives!

Excalibur

For a few months shy of ten years I worked for Excalibur Youth Services, which served emotionally troubled youth. As with any organization devoted to serving this population, there were hard days, there were sad days and there were glad days.

People often ask me if I enjoyed working with those kids. My response has always been, "I think that was the best job I ever had outside of my ministry. I got to help these guys turn their lives around, and I will never regret it. "

Some people tell me that those kids will never remember me after they have left Excalibur. They are wrong, though. I do keep in contact with a lot of them, and we continue encouraging one another. (Yes, it goes both ways.)

Just today, as I am writing this, I received this message from one of my Excalibur kids. He wrote, "Hey, I don't really have anyone to share my good news with, so here it goes. I finally got my GED and started college yesterday. I had to tell someone."

I won't identify this guy. He will always be a close friend. He endured what we had to put him through. He stood the test, and he has done well. Still, not having anyone to share his good news with, he remembered an old guy who really cared about him—and still does.

To him I say, "Thank you ever so much for sharing your story with me. You have proven yourself and have won the race many thought you were destined to lose. I always knew you had a winner's heart inside that stubborn shell. You never fooled me even on some of your bad days. Hang in there, kid! The world is yours! "

I have always said that you can never go wrong working with kids.

Wally Amidon

Veteran's Day 2010

My eyes are growing a little dimmer, and gray is beginning to streak my hair. My laugh lines are turning into small wrinkles now, and time is trying to slow me down some. I have gotten to live in this great country of ours for the past 60 years. I have experienced wars, riots, social turmoil, a presidential assassination, government corruption, and the resignations of a vice president and a president. I have seen my fellow citizens split by the color of their skin. Our country endured throughout all of that and will continue to be the greatest nation in the world because of those who love and support her and those who have given the ultimate sacrifice—their lives—for her.

Growing up in America as a teenager in the 1960s was a lot different than it is today. There was unrest in the streets because of a war raging in the swamps and mountains of a little country called Vietnam. The future wasn't bright in those days for all of us who were quickly approaching the age of 18. There was a draft in the country at that time, and 18-year-olds were some of the first to go. There were some who protested, burned their draft cards or our flag, and ran off to Canada to avoid serving in the military. They were a small minority, though. The young people of our country were fighting a foreign war in a faraway land, yet they endured.

I signed up in 1969. The United States government was using any available young person to fill the ranks of the military in those days. My buddies and I all signed up, giving over our lives as a blank check for our country to cash when needed. Some of my buddies' checks were cashed in; they never returned from those muddy rice paddies and jungles. The days of our laughter from doing together the things we enjoyed were suddenly torn apart, and the laughter was silenced. Only a pleasant memory of a day spent with that friend remains. The thought of friends who never returned still haunts my memories. These friends were cut down in the prime of their lives. Many never got to be old enough to get married and have a family or experience the American dream of buying and owning their own house. They gave up their lives so that you who sit here today will be able to enjoy those freedoms.

They were just kids, ranging in age from 17 to 19. They had the same dreams you have today. They wanted to live free and be able to live a normal life. Yet, war came, and they chose to set those dreams aside, hoping they would return and pick up where they left off. Many were able to return; some did not. Some of those who returned came home mutilated by the treacheries of war. Body parts were missing, and the horrors of war were still raging in their heads, causing some of them to be traumatized by life. Yet, they came back and tried to fit into mainstream America.

When they returned, they did not return to a hero's welcome as soldiers do today. Wearing a uniform in those days could cause you some problems. There were those would spit on you and call you a "warmonger" or a "baby killer." Yet, we wore our uniforms with pride. Mine still hangs in my closet with all the stripes and ribbons I earned in the four years I spent as a forward air controller in the Air Force.

I waited my turn in the rotation to go to Southeast Asia and do my part in the conflict, but that day never came for me. I was never called upon to go, but I watched some of my buddies go and then waited for them to return. It is a hard thing to be a teenager, to be a sergeant in the military, and to have to watch a friend be buried while "Taps" is being played on a bugle across the cemetery. The rifles roar to life, firing a 21-gun salute as your friend is laid to rest when he is only a few months past his 18th birthday. The flag is folded and handed to his sobbing mother as she is being told that the American people thank her for the sacrifice her son has made for his country. I always wondered if the parents heard those words as they watched their sons being buried.

There are people today who will not say the words to the "Pledge of Allegiance" to our flag. They stand with a closed mouth, not caring that my buddies gave their lives so that they can stand there with a closed mouth in a free country and not honor the flag my friends died for. There are others who choose not to stand when our National Anthem is played. When I attend a parade and see the flag coming, I take off my hat and, as a former serviceman, salute that flag as it goes by. I look around me and see others with hats still on their heads and just carrying on as if nothing special were going on before them. If the spirits of my slain buddies could shed a tear, I am sure there would be many shed for some of the thankless people we have in our country today.

I fly the American flag proudly from a 20-foot pole in front of my house. I look upon the 13 stripes that represent the original 13 colonies of our great nation and those who gave what they had to start the progress of freedom for the citizens of this country. The 50 stars represent the states that make up this wonderful union that we call America. I look upon my flag and think of what that banner represents. I look at my life and the lives of my buddies, those living and those who made the supreme sacrifice, and wonder if it was worth it all. My heart swells within me, pride fills my soul as I watch that flag fluttering in the gentle breeze, and I say a silent prayer for my fallen comrades: "Yes, yes, it was worth it all." God bless America!

At the VA Clinic

While at the Veterans Administration (VA) clinic recently, I came up behind an older man in a wheelchair. He was slowly wheeling his way through the corridor. Every now and then, he would stop and rub his hands together. It seemed to me that he had pain in his hand.

While he was stopped the next time, I came up behind him and asked him if I could use his wheelchair as a walker to get to the front desk. That way we both could get to where we were going with less time and pain involved. I told him my knees were killing me, walking on those hard, marble floors. I had no pain, but I knew this old war horse was very independent and wasn't going to allow someone to push him as long as he had strength enough to roll himself about.

We got to the main desk, and I asked him if this is where he needed to be. He said it was, and he thanked me for helping him along as I used his wheelchair for a walker.

As I walked away, he said, "I know you don't have pain in your knees and that you never needed me and my chair to help you along. I am starting to get arthritis in my hands now, and sometimes it is hard for me to wheel myself around. I really was having a hard time back there, and then you came along with that flimsy excuse of yours to help me get up here. It is hard for me to realize that I am an old man now and that having to get help is going to be inevitable from now on. Thank you, young fella."

He called me "young fella." "How old are you?" I asked him.

He smiled and said, "I'm going on 33 for the third time."

He was almost 99, and he was in a wheel chair, saying he was getting arthritis at his age. I see now why his group was called "the Greatest Generation."

As I turned to leave, he said, "Thank you for your service—for when you were in and for your service today."

I turned and walked back to him and gave him a big old bear hug. I told him it was great to know a real hero.

It's the little things in life like this that keep me happy. Meeting this man and talking with fellow veterans keep life real for me.

West Virginia Lottery Winners

Wheeling, WV. (AP News). Eight West Virginia women stepped forward today to claim the $276 million Powerball lottery prize. The women, who wanted to remain anonymous, bought the ticket at a local bar they frequented after work. When asked what they planned to do with their new-found wealth, they answered in the following manner:

Winner #1 – "I plan on quittin' my job at the coal mine and go see the rest of the world. I'm gonna cross the county line tomorrow and see what's just over them hills."

Winner #2 – "I gonna git some front teeth. Hate trying to eat or sip corn without front teeth. Have to mash ever-thin' with my three back teeth and that gits a might hard at times."

Winner #3 – "I'm gonna build my own still. Hate payin' the middle man."

Winner #4 – "Me and my boyfriend are gonna make it legal and get married. I don't care if he is my uncle."

Winner #5 – "I'm building a new outhouse closer to the cabin. Hate walkin' barefoot out to the outhouse, especially when it's snowing out."

Winner #6 – "I might git me a new mule. The one we got now is plum wore out. Just might git two of them critters so we can git the fields plowed twiced as fast."

Winner #7 – "I'm gonna buy a whole truckload of flour so I can use the sacks to make me a bunch of new dresses and curtains for the kitchen."

Winner #8 – "I'm putting one of them OnStar systems on the mule in case we go over the cliff. I, at least, want Momma to know where I'm at."

When asked what they thought about being celebrities, one of the women answered, "Now, that's downright personal. What we do with our men and cousins is our business."

The governor is due to arrive Wednesday to present the check and to propose to at least four of the winners.

What Is a Redneck?

It would be hard to define what a real redneck is. Any part of this country of ours has localized versions of what would constitute being a redneck. To me, a redneck is someone who doesn't let the cares of the world drag him down. He doesn't like to make waves and just wishes the world would go by with all of its problems and not involve him. He is a happy person who likes fun, is not politically correct, and will defend his right to be himself if others try to intervene and try to change him or her ways.

He doesn't care that others outside of his social circle ostracize him for the things he does, the way he acts, or how he thinks. He himself is a free thinker, that being he doesn't align himself with popular movements, social circles, or any other thing that would draw attention to him or let others think he is something he really isn't.

He is a humble person who doesn't ty to keep up with others, the world, or the changes politicans try to bring into this world. His idea of fun is doing something local and not trying to outdo his neighbor for he is there to help him.

This person labeled as a redneck is probably looked down upon by those who think they are something they really aren't, who live above their means, and who wouldn't do anything for their fellow human unless it involved something that they could get out of it for themselves.

Rednecks are fun-loving people whom others think live in their own little world, not worrying if the world is going to collapse around them because everything in their little world is running smoothly because they make it happen that way.

There are people who have to take medicine to calm their nerves, see a psychiatrist on a regular basis, have to have counseling to exist in this world, and just plain are not happy with their lot in this old world of ours. There is a simple cure for shot nerves, broken spirits, and not loving life: be what you label others and then think that being yourself is not all that bad.

Have fun! Love life, and live it to its fullest! Then, if somebody labels you a redneck or calls you by any other geographical name, it will not bother you for now you know that you are not the person with the problems.

If you are ever driving through the deep South and see the Stars and Bars hanging from a pole in front of a house, whether it be a single-wide trailer or a mansion with finely groomed lawns, don't look upon that banner as a "rebel flag" for it is not. It is not a symbol of racism, as many try to promote today, but it is the symbol of that person's heritage from a bygone time, a heritage this person refuses to give up in the name of what some call "progress" and the homogenization of America. If you look about you, you may also see the American flag fluttering proudly in the breeze, another symbol of this same heritage that this person refuses to let others take from him.

Yes, my friend, this is a great country we live in today. Rednecks and others like them have been the backbone of American progress and have made this the greatest country in the free world. From the coal miners of Appalachia to the explorers of the wild western frontier, those who took a chance on life and sought out the simple ways gave us what we have today. I can never think of myself as better than any of them.

Living free and being able to do as you please within the limits of the law is the rule of the redneck. Some may not like their way of life, but so be it. As they say in the hills of New Hampshire where I come from, "Ayuh, it ain't that I feel lost livin' out heah. It's gittin' found that bothahs me."

The End
. . . for now

Selected Books by MSI Press

CPSIA information can be obtained at www.ICGtesting.com
Printed in the USA
BVOW04s1800120215

387313BV00012B/426/P